Love Food ® is an imprint of Parragon Books Ltd

Parragon
Queen Street House
4 Queen Street
Bath BA1 1HE, UK

Copyright © Parragon Books Ltd 2006
Designed by Terry Jeavons & Company

Love Food ® and the accompanying heart device is a trademark of Parragon Books
Ltd

ISBN 978-1-4075-3961-4

Printed in Indonesia

This book uses imperial, metric, and US cup measurements. Follow the same units of
measurement throughout; do not mix imperial and metric. All spoon measurements are
level, unless otherwise stated: teaspoons are assumed to be 5ml, and tablespoons are
assumed to be 15ml. Unless otherwise stated, milk is assumed to be whole, eggs and
individual fruits such as bananas are medium, and pepper is freshly ground black
pepper.

Recipes using raw or very lightly cooked eggs should be avoided by infants, the elderly,
pregnant women, convalescents, and anyone suffering from an illness. Pregnant and
breast-feeding women are advised to avoid eating peanuts and peanut products.

spanish

introduction

The cuisine of Spain is influenced by many things, not least of which is its wonderful position with endless miles of coastline on the Mediterranean Sea and the Atlantic Ocean. Add to this plenty of fresh, top-quality, locally grown seasonal produce, an appreciation of well-prepared food, and a tradition of hospitality and generosity, and it is little wonder that there are many superb dishes in the Spanish cook's repertoire.

The country's history has also left its mark on the nation's cuisine. Early invaders introduced grapevines and olive trees, while the Arabian Moors developed extensive irrigation systems to

support the crops they brought with them. Many of the foods associated with modern Spain—rice, citrus fruits, dates, apricots, peaches, almonds, and eggplants—are a legacy of the Moorish conquest.

In the 15th century, the explorer Christopher Columbus completed the list of healthy ingredients that makes up the Mediterranean diet with his discovery in the Caribbean Islands of colorful hot and sweet peppers.

Columbus also brought cocoa beans, although it was later in the 16th century that Hernán Cortés brought chocolate-making equipment from Mexico, sparking a passion for chocolate that has survived to this day. The much-loved Spanish breakfast of deep-fried pastries, churros, is served with glasses of thick hot chocolate. The long tradition of daily market shopping for fresh fruit, vegetables, and seafood still continues, and market days in rural communities are as important as ever, with vendors selling seafood of all kinds, both freshly butchered and preserved meats, and of course the fruit and vegetables that grow so well here.

A little taste of Spain's fascinating heritage is contained in the delicious recipes in this book—so step back in time as you eat and enjoy!

tapas

Eating tapas epitomizes the Spanish way of life—relaxed, sociable, friendly, with the focus on seasonal foods presented in bite-size pieces that go beautifully with a glass of chilled beer, white wine, or sherry. Why bite-size? Well, it seems that tapas evolved from an innkeeper's custom of putting a lid, *tapa*, in the form of a slice of bread, on a customer's wine glass to keep out the flies and dust. Someone then came up with the idea of balancing a little morsel of something tasty on top of the bread to nibble on—perhaps a cube or two of cheese or ham—and within a very short time, the tapas bar was born. The morsels became more innovative and sophisticated and now tapas are made from a wonderful variety of foods—meat, seafood, eggs, nuts, and cheese, as well as vibrant Mediterranean vegetables, with a wonderful array of dips and sauces to accompany.

The numbers of servings indicated in this chapter assume that you are making the recipe as part of a tapas meal. Some of the recipes, such as Tiny Spanish Meatballs in Almond Sauce, can be served as a light lunch or supper dish, with some crusty bread and a crisp green salad to accompany—simply increase the quantities of ingredients as appropriate, or use the same quantities to serve fewer people.

salted almonds

ingredients

SERVES 6–8

8 oz/225 g/scant 1¹/₂ cups
    whole almonds, in their
    skins

4 tbsp Spanish olive oil

coarse sea salt

1 tsp paprika or ground
    cumin (optional)

method

1 Put the almonds in a bowl, cover with boiling water for 3–4 minutes, then plunge them into cold water for 1 minute. Drain them well in a strainer, then slide off the skins between your fingers. Dry the almonds well on paper towels.

2 Put the olive oil in a roasting pan and swirl it round so that it covers the bottom. Add the almonds and toss them in the pan so that they are evenly coated in the oil, then spread them out in a single layer.

3 Roast the almonds in a preheated oven, 350°F/180°C, for 20 minutes, or until they are light golden brown, tossing several times during the cooking. Drain the almonds on paper towels, then transfer them to a bowl.

4 While the almonds are still warm, sprinkle with plenty of sea salt and the paprika or cumin, if using, and toss well together to coat. Serve the almonds immediately or let cool completely. The almonds are at their best when served freshly cooked, but they can be stored in an airtight container for up to 3 days.

olives wrapped with anchovies

ingredients

MAKES 12

12 anchovy fillets in oil, drained

24 pimiento-stuffed green olives in oil, drained

method

1 Thinly slice each anchovy fillet lengthwise. Wrap a half fillet round the center of each olive, overlapping the ends, and secure with a wooden toothpick. Repeat with another olive and anchovy fillet half and slide onto the toothpick.

2 Continue until all the ingredients are used, and you have 12 pinchons with 2 anchovy-wrapped olives on each toothpick.

cracked marinated olives

ingredients

SERVES 8

1 lb/450 g can or jar unpitted
large green olives, drained

4 garlic cloves, peeled

2 tsp coriander seeds

1 small lemon

4 sprigs of fresh thyme

4 feathery stalks of fennel

2 small fresh red chiles
(optional)

pepper

Spanish extra-virgin olive oil,
to cover

method

1 To allow the flavors of the marinade to penetrate the olives, place on a cutting board and, using a rolling pin, bash them lightly so that they crack slightly. Alternatively, use a sharp knife to cut a lengthwise slit in each olive as far as the pit. Using the flat side of a broad knife, lightly crush each garlic clove. Using a mortar and pestle, crack the coriander seeds. Cut the lemon, with its rind, into small chunks.

2 Put the olives, garlic, coriander seeds, lemon chunks, thyme sprigs, fennel, and chiles, if using, in a large bowl and toss together. Season with pepper to taste, but you should not need to add salt as preserved olives are usually salty enough. Pack the ingredients tightly into a glass jar with a lid. Pour in enough olive oil to cover the olives, then seal the jar tightly.

3 Let the olives stand at room temperature for 24 hours, then marinate in the refrigerator for at least 1 week but preferably 2 weeks before serving. From time to time, gently give the jar a shake to remix the ingredients. Return the olives to room temperature and remove from the oil to serve. Provide toothpicks for spearing the olives.

broiled eggplant dip

ingredients

SERVES 6–8

1 large eggplant,
  about 14 oz/400 g
olive oil
2 scallions, chopped finely
1 large garlic clove, crushed
2 tbsp finely chopped
  fresh parsley
salt and pepper
smoked sweet Spanish paprika,
  to garnish
French bread, to serve

method

1 Heat 4 tablespoons of the oil in a large skillet over medium-high heat. Add the eggplant slices and cook on both sides until soft and starting to brown. Remove from the skillet and set aside to cool. The slices will release the oil again as they cool.

2 Heat another tablespoon of oil in the skillet. Add the onions and garlic and cook for 3 minutes, or until the scallions become soft. Remove from the heat and set aside with the eggplant slices to cool.

3 Transfer all the ingredients to a food processor and process just until a coarse purée forms. Transfer to a serving bowl and stir in the parsley. Taste and adjust the seasoning, if necessary. Serve at once, or cover and let chill until 15 minutes before required. Sprinkle with paprika and serve with slices of French bread.

moorish fava bean dip

ingredients

SERVES 6

1 lb 2 oz/500 g shelled fresh
  or frozen fava beans

5 tbsp olive oil

1 garlic clove, finely chopped

1 onion, finely chopped

1 tsp ground cumin

1 tbsp lemon juice

6 fl oz/175 ml/$^3/_4$ cup water

1 tbsp chopped fresh mint

salt and pepper

paprika, to garnish

raw vegetables, crusty bread
  or breadsticks, to serve

method

1 If using fresh fava beans, bring a large pan of lightly salted water to a boil. Add the beans, then reduce the heat and simmer, covered, for 7 minutes. Drain well, then refresh under cold running water and drain again. Remove and discard the outer skins. If using frozen beans, let thaw completely, then remove and discard the outer skins.

2 Heat 1 tablespoon of the olive oil in a skillet. Add the garlic, onion, and cumin and cook over low heat, stirring occasionally, until the onion is softened and translucent. Add the fava beans and cook, stirring frequently, for 5 minutes.

3 Remove the skillet from the heat and transfer the mixture to a food processor or blender. Add the lemon juice, the remaining olive oil, water, and mint and process to a paste. Season to taste with salt and pepper.

4 Scrape the paste back into the skillet and heat gently until warm. Transfer to individual serving bowls and dust lightly with paprika. Serve with dippers of your choice.

tiny spanish meatballs in almond sauce

ingredients

SERVES 6–8

2 oz/55 g white or brown
bread, crusts removed,
broken into small pieces

3 tbsp water

1 lb/250 g/2 cups fresh lean
ground pork

1 large onion, finely chopped

1 garlic clove, crushed

2 tbsp chopped fresh flat-leaf
parsley, plus extra to garnish

1 egg, beaten

freshly grated nutmeg

salt and pepper

flour, for coating

2 tbsp Spanish olive oil

squeeze of lemon juice

almond sauce

2 tbsp Spanish olive oil

1 oz/25 g white or brown bread

4 oz/115 g/^{2}/$_3$ cup blanched
almonds

2 garlic cloves, finely chopped

5 fl oz/150 ml/^{2}/$_3$ cup
dry white wine

salt and pepper

15 fl oz/425 ml/scant 2 cups
vegetable stock

method

1 To prepare the meatballs, put the bread in a bowl, add the water, and let soak for 5 minutes. Squeeze out the water and return the bread to the dried bowl. Add the pork, onion, garlic, parsley, and egg, then season with grated nutmeg and a little salt and pepper. Knead well to form a smooth mixture.

2 Spread some flour on a plate. With floured hands, shape the meat mixture into about 30 equal-size balls, then roll each meatball in flour until coated. Heat the olive oil in a large, heavy-bottom skillet and cook the meatballs, in batches, for 4–5 minutes, or until browned all over. Remove from the skillet and set aside.

3 To make the almond sauce, heat the olive oil in the skillet. Add the bread with the almonds and cook gently, stirring, until golden. Add the garlic and cook for 30 seconds, then add the wine and boil for 1–2 minutes. Season to taste and let cool. Whiz in a food processor with the stock until smooth. Return to the skillet.

4 Carefully add the cooked meatballs to the almond sauce and let simmer for 25 minutes, or until the meatballs are tender. Transfer the meatballs and almond sauce to a serving dish, then add a squeeze of lemon juice to taste and sprinkle with chopped parsley to garnish.

chorizo in red wine

ingredients

SERVES 6

7 oz/200 g chorizo sausage

7 fl oz/200 ml/generous
   3/4 cup Spanish red wine

2 tbsp brandy (optional)

fresh flat-leaf parsley sprigs,
   to garnish

crusty bread, to serve

method

1 Using a fork, prick the chorizo in 3 or 4 places. Place in a large pan and pour the wine over. Bring the wine to a boil, then reduce the heat and simmer gently, covered, for 15–20 minutes. Transfer the chorizo and wine to a bowl or dish, cover and let the sausage marinate overnight.

2 The next day, remove the chorizo from the bowl or dish and reserve the wine. Remove the outer casing from the chorizo and cut the sausage into 1/4-inch/5-mm slices. Place the slices in a large, heavy-bottom skillet or flameproof serving dish.

3 If you are adding the brandy, pour it into a small pan and heat gently. Pour the brandy over the chorizo slices, then stand well back and set alight. When the flames have died down, shake the pan gently and add the reserved wine to the pan, then cook over high heat until almost all of the wine has evaporated.

4 Serve the chorizo in red wine piping hot, in the dish in which it was cooked, sprinkled with parsley to garnish. Accompany with chunks or slices of bread to mop up the juices and provide wooden toothpicks to spear the pieces of chorizo.

chorizo empanadillas

ingredients

MAKES 12

4½ oz/125 g chorizo
    sausage, outer casing
    removed
all-purpose flour, for dusting
9 oz/250 g ready-made puff
    pastry, thawed if frozen
beaten egg, to glaze
paprika, to garnish

method

1 Cut the chorizo sausage into small dice measuring about ½ inch/1 cm square.

2 On a lightly floured counter, thinly roll out the puff pastry. Using a plain, round 3¼-inch/8-cm cutter, cut into circles. Gently pile the trimmings together, roll out again, then cut out additional circles to produce 12 in total. Put about a teaspoonful of the chopped chorizo onto each of the pastry circles.

3 Dampen the edges of the pastry with a little water, then fold one half over the other half to completely cover the chorizo. Seal the edges together with your fingers. Using the prongs of a fork, press against the edges to give a decorative finish and seal them further. With the tip of a sharp knife, make a small slit in the side of each pastry. You can store the pastries in the refrigerator at this stage until you are ready to bake them.

4 Place the pastries onto dampened baking sheets and brush each with a little beaten egg to glaze. Bake in a preheated oven, 400°F/200°C, for 10–15 minutes, or until golden brown and puffed. Using a small strainer, lightly dust the top of each empanadilla with a little paprika to garnish. Serve the chorizo empanadillas hot or warm.

bandilleras

ingredients

SERVES 18

1 tbsp white wine vinegar

4 garlic cloves, finely chopped

1 fresh red chile, seeded and
finely chopped

1 tbsp sweet paprika

4 tbsp olive oil

3 skinless, boneless chicken
breasts, cut into 1-inch/
2.5-cm cubes

1 avocado

3 tbsp lemon juice

4 oz/115 g San Simon or other
smoked cheese, diced

8–10 black olives, pitted

8–10 cherry tomatoes

3 oz/85 g Manchego or
Cheddar cheese, cubed

8–10 pimiento-stuffed
green olives

1/2 cantaloupe melon, seeded

5–6 slices serrano ham

picada

4 garlic cloves, finely chopped

6 tbsp chopped fresh parsley

6 tbsp pickled cucumber,
finely chopped

5 fl oz/150 ml/2/3 cup olive oil

method

1 Mix the vinegar, garlic, chile, paprika, and olive oil together in a bowl. Add the chicken and stir well to coat, then cover and let marinate in the refrigerator for at least 2 hours or preferably overnight.

2 Heat a large, heavy-bottom skillet. Tip the chicken mixture into the pan and cook over low heat, stirring frequently, for 10–15 minutes, or until cooked through. Remove from the heat and let cool to room temperature, then spear the chicken pieces with wooden toothpicks.

3 Peel and stone the avocado and cut into bite-size cubes. Toss in the lemon juice, then thread onto wooden toothpicks with the smoked cheese. Thread the black olives, tomatoes, Manchego cheese, and stuffed olives onto wooden toothpicks.

4 Scoop out 20 balls from the melon with a melon baller or teaspoon. Cut the ham into 20 strips and wrap around the melon balls. Thread the melon balls in pairs onto wooden toothpicks.

5 To make the picada, mix all the ingredients together in a bowl until thoroughly combined into a fairly thick paste.

6 Arrange the bandilleras on a large serving platter and serve with bowls of picada.

chicken in lemon & garlic

ingredients

SERVES 6–8

4 large skinless, boneless
chicken breasts
5 tbsp Spanish olive oil
1 onion, finely chopped
6 garlic cloves, finely chopped
grated rind of 1 lemon, finely
pared rind of 1 lemon and
juice of both lemons
4 tbsp chopped fresh flat-leaf
parsley, plus extra
to garnish
salt and pepper
lemon wedges and crusty
bread, to serve

method

1 Using a sharp knife, slice the chicken breasts widthwise into very thin slices. Heat the olive oil in a large, heavy-bottom skillet, add the onion and cook for 5 minutes, or until softened but not browned. Add the garlic and cook for an additional 30 seconds.

2 Add the sliced chicken to the skillet and cook gently for 5–10 minutes, stirring from time to time, until all the ingredients are lightly browned and the chicken is tender.

3 Add the grated lemon rind and the lemon juice and let it bubble. At the same time, deglaze the skillet by scraping and stirring all the bits on the bottom of the skillet into the juices with a wooden spoon. Remove the skillet from the heat, stir in the parsley, and season to taste with salt and pepper.

4 Transfer the chicken in lemon and garlic, piping hot, to a warmed serving dish. Sprinkle with the pared lemon rind, garnish with the parsley, and serve with lemon wedges for squeezing over the chicken, accompanied by chunks or slices of crusty bread for mopping up the lemon and garlic juices.

salt cod fritters with spinach

ingredients

MAKES ABOUT 16

9 oz/250 g dried salt cod
in 1 piece

batter
5 oz/140 g/scant 1 cup
all-purpose flour
1 tsp baking powder
$^{1}/_{4}$ tsp salt
1 large egg, beaten lightly
about 5 fl oz/150 ml/
$^{2}/_{3}$ cup milk

2 lemon slices
2 fresh parsley sprigs
1 bay leaf
$^{1}/_{2}$ tbsp garlic-flavored olive oil
3 oz/85 g/scant 2 cups baby
spinach, rinsed
$^{1}/_{4}$ tsp smoked sweet, mild, or
hot Spanish paprika, to taste
olive oil
1 quantity garlic mayonnaise,
to serve (see page 200)

method

1 Place the dried salt cod in a large bowl, cover with cold water, and let soak for 48 hours, changing the water at least 3 times.

2 To make the batter, sift the flour, baking powder, and salt into a large bowl and make a well. Mix the egg with 4 fl oz/125 ml/generous $^{1}/_{3}$ cup of the milk and pour into the well, stirring to make a smooth batter with a thick coating consistency. Stir in the remaining milk if it seems too thick. Set aside for 1 hour.

3 Transfer the soaked salt cod to a large skillet. Add the lemon slices, parsley sprigs, bay leaf, and enough water to cover and bring to a boil. Reduce the heat and let simmer for 30–45 minutes, or until the fish flakes easily.

4 Heat the oil in a small pan over medium heat. Add the spinach with the rinsing water clinging to its leaves and cook for 3–4 minutes until wilted. Drain and press out any excess water. Finely chop the spinach, then stir it into the batter with the paprika. Drain the fish and flake the flesh into fine pieces, removing all the skin and tiny bones. Stir into the batter.

5 Heat 2 inches/5 cm of oil in a heavy-bottom skillet to 375°F/190°C. Use a greased tablespoon to drop spoonfuls of the batter, in batches, into the oil. Cook for 8–10 minutes until golden brown. Drain the fritters on paper towels and serve with garlic mayonnaise.

calamares

ingredients

SERVES 6

1 lb/450 g prepared squid

all-purpose flour, for coating

corn oil, for deep-frying

salt

lemon wedges, to garnish

aïoli, to serve (see page 44)

method

1 Slice the squid into 1/2-inch/1-cm rings and halve the tentacles if large. Rinse and dry well on paper towels so that they do not spit during cooking. Dust the squid rings with flour so that they are lightly coated. Do not season the flour, as this will toughen the squid.

2 Put the corn oil in a deep-fryer and heat to 350–375°F/180–190°C, or until a cube of bread browns in 30 seconds. Carefully add the squid rings in batches, so that the temperature of the oil does not drop, and deep-fry for 2–3 minutes, or until golden brown and crisp all over, turning several times. Do not overcook as the squid will become tough and rubbery rather than moist and tender.

3 Using a slotted spoon, remove the deep-fried squid from the deep-fryer and drain well on paper towels. Transfer to a warm oven while you deep-fry the remaining squid rings.

4 Sprinkle the deep-fried squid with salt and serve piping hot, garnished with lemon wedges for squeezing over them. Accompany with a bowl of aïoli in which to dip the pieces.

sizzling chile shrimp

ingredients

SERVES 8

1 lb 2 oz/500 g raw jumbo
     shrimp, in their shells
1 small fresh red chile
6 tbsp Spanish olive oil
2 garlic cloves, finely chopped
pinch of paprika
salt
crusty bread, to serve

method

1 To prepare the shrimp, pull off their heads. With your fingers, peel off their shells, leaving the tails intact. Using a sharp knife, make a shallow slit along the back or outside of each shrimp, then pull out the dark vein and discard. Rinse the shrimp under cold water and dry well on paper towels.

2 Cut the chile in half lengthwise, remove the seeds, and finely chop the flesh. It is important either to wear gloves or to wash your hands very thoroughly after chopping chiles because their juices can cause irritation to sensitive skin, especially round the eyes, nose, or mouth.

3 Heat the olive oil in a large, heavy-bottom skillet or ovenproof casserole until quite hot, then add the garlic and cook for 30 seconds. Add the shrimp, chile, paprika, and a pinch of salt and cook for 2–3 minutes, stirring, until the shrimp turn pink and start to curl.

4 Serve the shrimp in the cooking dish, still sizzling. Accompany with toothpicks, to spear the shrimp, and chunks or slices of crusty bread to mop up the aromatic cooking oil.

mussels with herb & garlic butter

ingredients

SERVES 8

1 lb 12 oz/800 g fresh mussels, in their shells

splash of dry white wine

1 bay leaf

3 oz/85 g butter

12 oz/350 g/generous 1/2 cup fresh white or brown bread crumbs

4 tbsp chopped fresh flat-leaf parsley, plus extra sprigs to garnish

2 tbsp snipped fresh chives

2 garlic cloves, finely chopped

salt and pepper

lemon wedges, to serve

method

1 Scrub the mussel shells under cold running water and pull off any beards. Discard any with broken shells. Tap the remaining mussels and discard any that refuse to close.

2 Put the mussels in a large pan and add the wine and the bay leaf. Cook, covered, over high heat for 5 minutes, shaking the pan occasionally, or until the mussels are opened. Drain the mussels and discard any that remain closed. Shell the mussels, reserving one half of each shell. Arrange the mussels, in their half shells, in a large, shallow, ovenproof serving dish.

3 Melt the butter and pour into a small bowl. Add the bread crumbs, parsley, chives, garlic, and salt and pepper to taste and mix well together. Let stand until the butter has set slightly. Using your fingers or 2 teaspoons, take a large pinch of the herb and butter mixture and use to fill each mussel shell, pressing it down well.

4 To serve, bake the mussels in a preheated oven, 450°F/230°C, for 10 minutes, or until hot. Serve immediately, garnished with parsley sprigs, and accompanied by lemon wedges for squeezing over them.

broiled sardines

ingredients

SERVES 4–6

2 tbsp garlic-flavored olive oil

12 fresh sardines, deheaded,
    cleaned, backbone removed

coarse sea salt and pepper

lemon wedges, to serve

method

1 Preheat the broiler to high and brush the broiler rack with a little of the garlic-flavored oil. Brush the sardines with the oil and arrange in a single layer on the broiler rack. Sprinkle with salt and pepper to taste.

2 Broil about 4 inches/10 cm from the heat for 3 minutes, or until the skin becomes crisp. Use kitchen tongs to turn the sardines over and brush with more oil and sprinkle with salt and pepper. Continue broiling for 2–3 minutes until the flesh flakes easily and the skin is crisp. Serve at once, with lemon wedges.

figs with bleu cheese

ingredients

SERVES 6

caramelized almonds

100 g/3^1/$_2$ oz/^{1}/$_2$ cup superfine sugar

4oz/115 g/generous ^{3}/$_4$ cup whole almonds, blanched or unblanched

12 ripe figs

12 oz/350 g Spanish bleu cheese, such as Picós, crumbled

extra-virgin olive oil

method

1 First make the caramelized almonds. Put the sugar in a pan over medium-high heat and stir until the sugar melts and turns golden brown and bubbles: do not stir once the mixture starts to bubble. Remove from the heat and add the almonds one at a time and quickly turn with a fork until coated; if the caramel hardens, return the pan to the heat. Transfer each almond to a lightly buttered baking sheet once it is coated. Let stand until cool and firm.

2 To serve, slice the figs in half and arrange 4 halves on each plate. Coarsely chop the almonds by hand. Place a mound of bleu cheese on each plate and sprinkle with chopped almonds. Drizzle the figs very lightly with the oil.

cheese puffs with fiery tomato salsa

ingredients

SERVES 8

2¹/₂ oz/70 g/scant ¹/₂ cup
  all-purpose flour
2 fl oz/50 ml/¹/₄ cup
  Spanish olive oil
5 fl oz/150 ml/²/₃ cup water
2 eggs, beaten
2 oz/55 g/¹/₂ cup Manchego,
  Parmesan, Cheddar,
  Gouda, or Gruyère cheese,
  finely grated
¹/₂ tsp paprika
salt and pepper
corn oil, for deep-frying

fiery tomato salsa
2 tbsp Spanish olive oil
1 small onion, finely chopped
1 garlic clove, crushed
splash of dry white wine
14 oz/400 g canned chopped
  tomatoes
1 tbsp tomato paste
¹/₄–¹/₂ tsp dried red
  pepper flakes
dash of Tabasco sauce
pinch of sugar
salt and pepper

method

1 To make the salsa, heat the olive oil in a pan, add the onion, and cook until softened but not browned. Add the garlic and cook for 30 seconds. Add the wine and let bubble, then add the remaining salsa ingredients and let simmer, uncovered, until a thick sauce is formed. Set aside until ready to serve.

2 Meanwhile, prepare the cheese puffs. Sift the flour onto a plate. Put the olive oil and water in a pan and slowly bring to a boil. As soon as the water boils, remove the pan from the heat, and quickly tip in the flour. Using a wooden spoon, beat the mixture well until it is smooth and leaves the sides of the pan.

3 Let cool for 1–2 minutes, then gradually add the eggs, beating hard after each addition and keeping the mixture stiff. Add the cheese and paprika, season to taste with salt and pepper, and mix well together.

4 To cook the cheese puffs, heat the corn oil in a deep-fryer to 350–375°F/180–190°C. Drop teaspoonfuls of the prepared mixture, in batches, into the hot oil and deep-fry for 2–3 minutes, turning once, or until golden and crispy. They should rise to the surface of the oil and puff up. Drain well on paper towels. Serve the puffs piping hot, with the fiery salsa.

deep-fried manchego cheese

ingredients

SERVES 6–8

7 oz/200 g Manchego cheese

3 tbsp all-purpose flour

salt and pepper

1 egg

1 tsp water

3 oz/85 g/1^1/$_2$ cups fresh
 white or brown bread
 crumbs

corn oil, for deep-frying

method

1 Slice the cheese into triangular shapes about ^{3}/$_4$ inch/2 cm thick or alternatively into cubes measuring about the same size. Put the flour in a plastic bag and season with salt and pepper to taste. Break the egg into a shallow dish and beat together with the water. Spread the bread crumbs onto a plate.

2 Coat the cheese pieces evenly in the flour, then dip the cheese in the egg mixture. Finally, dip the cheese in the bread crumbs so that the pieces are coated on all sides. Transfer to a large plate and store in the refrigerator until you are ready to serve them.

3 Just before serving, heat the oil in a deep-fryer to 350–375°F/180–190°C. If the oil is not hot enough, the coating on the cheese will take too long to become crisp and the cheese inside may ooze out. Add the cheese pieces, in batches of 4 or 5 pieces so that the temperature of the oil does not drop, and deep-fry for 1–2 minutes, turning once, until the cheese is just starting to melt and they are golden brown on all sides.

4 Using a slotted spoon, remove the deep-fried cheese from the skillet or deep-fryer and drain well on paper towels. Serve the deep-fried cheese pieces hot.

baby potatoes with aïoli

ingredients

SERVES 6–8

1 lb/450 g baby new potatoes

1 tbsp chopped fresh
    flat-leaf parsley

salt

aïoli

1 large egg yolk, at room
    temperature

1 tbsp white wine vinegar or
    lemon juice

2 large garlic cloves, peeled

salt and pepper

5 tbsp Spanish extra-virgin
    olive oil

5 tbsp corn oil

method

1 To make the aïoli, blend the egg yolk, vinegar, garlic, and salt and pepper to taste in a food processor. With the motor still running, very slowly add the olive oil, then the corn oil, drop by drop at first, then, when it starts to thicken, in a slow, steady stream until the sauce is thick and smooth. Alternatively, mix in a bowl with a whisk. Quickly blend in 1 tablespoon of water so that the aïoli forms the consistency of sauce.

2 To prepare the potatoes, cut them in half or fourths to make bite-size pieces. If they are very small, you can leave them whole. Put the potatoes in a large pan of cold, salted water and bring to a boil. Lower the heat and let simmer for 7 minutes, or until just tender. Drain well, then turn out into a large bowl.

3 While the potatoes are still warm, pour over the aïoli sauce, and gently toss the potatoes in it. Adding the sauce to the potatoes while they are still warm will help them to absorb the garlic flavor. Let stand for about 20 minutes to allow the potatoes to marinate in the sauce.

4 Transfer the potatoes with aïoli to a warmed serving dish, sprinkle over the parsley and salt to taste, and serve warm.

roasted asparagus with serrano ham

ingredients

MAKES 12

2 tbsp Spanish olive oil

6 slices serrano ham

12 asparagus spears

pepper

garlic mayonnaise, to serve
(see page 200)

method

1 Put half the olive oil in a roasting pan that will hold the asparagus spears in a single layer and swirl it round so that it covers the bottom. Cut the slices of serrano ham in half lengthwise.

2 Trim the ends of the asparagus spears, then wrap a slice of ham round the stem end of each spear. Place the wrapped spears in the prepared roasting pan and lightly brush the ham and asparagus with the remaining olive oil. Season the spears with pepper.

3 Roast in a preheated oven, 400°F/200°C, for 10 minutes, depending on the thickness of the asparagus, or until tender but still firm. Do not overcook the asparagus spears as it is important that they are still firm.

4 Serve piping hot, accompanied by a bowl of garlic mayonnaise for dipping.

zucchini fritters with pine nut sauce

ingredients

SERVES 8

1 lb/450 g baby zucchini

3 tbsp all-purpose flour

1 tsp paprika

1 large egg

2 tbsp milk

corn oil, for pan-frying

coarse sea salt

pine nut sauce

3 $\frac{1}{2}$ oz/100 g/generous
    $\frac{1}{2}$ cup pine nuts

1 garlic clove, peeled

3 tbsp Spanish extra-virgin
    olive oil

1 tbsp lemon juice

3 tbsp water

1 tbsp chopped fresh
    flat-leaf parsley

salt and pepper

method

1 Put the pine nuts and garlic in a food processor and blend to form a purée. With the motor still running, gradually add the olive oil, lemon juice, and water to form a smooth sauce. Stir in the parsley and season to taste with salt and pepper. Turn into a serving bowl.

2 To prepare the zucchini, cut them on the diagonal into thin slices about $\frac{1}{4}$ inch/5 mm thick. Put the flour and paprika in a plastic bag and mix together. Beat the egg and milk together in a large bowl.

3 Add the zucchini slices to the flour mixture and toss well together until coated. Shake off the excess flour. Pour enough corn oil into a large, heavy-bottom skillet for a depth of about $\frac{1}{2}$ inch/1 cm, and heat. Dip the zucchini slices, one at a time, into the egg mixture, then slip them into the hot oil. Cook the zucchini slices, in batches of a single layer, for 2 minutes, or until crisp and golden brown.

4 Using a slotted spoon, remove the fritters from the skillet and drain on paper towels. Continue until all the zucchini slices have been cooked.

5 Serve the zucchini fritters piping hot, lightly sprinkled with sea salt. Accompany with the pine nut sauce.

garlic tomatoes

ingredients

SERVES 6

8 deep red tomatoes

3 fresh thyme sprigs,
    plus extra to garnish

12 garlic cloves, unpeeled

2$^1/_2$ fl oz/75 ml/generous
    $^1/_4$ cup olive oil

salt and pepper

method

1 Cut the tomatoes in half lengthwise and arrange, cut-side up, in a single layer in a large, ovenproof dish. Tuck the thyme sprigs and garlic cloves between them.

2 Drizzle the olive oil all over the tomatoes and season to taste with pepper. Bake in a preheated oven, 425°F/220°C, for 40–45 minutes, or until the tomatoes are softened and beginning to char around the edges.

3 Remove and discard the thyme sprigs. Season the tomatoes to taste with salt and pepper. Garnish with the extra thyme sprigs and serve hot or warm. Squeeze the pulp from the garlic over the tomatoes at the table.

sautéed garlic mushrooms

ingredients

SERVES 6

1 lb/450 g white mushrooms

5 tbsp Spanish olive oil

2 garlic cloves, finely chopped

squeeze of lemon juice

salt and pepper

4 tbsp chopped fresh
    flat-leaf parsley

crusty bread, to serve

method

1 Wipe or brush clean the mushrooms, then trim off the stalks close to the caps. Cut any large mushrooms in half or into fourths. Heat the olive oil in a large, heavy-bottom skillet, add the garlic and cook for 30 seconds–1 minute, or until lightly browned. Add the mushrooms and sauté over high heat, stirring most of the time, until the mushrooms have absorbed all the oil in the skillet.

2 Reduce the heat to low. When the juices have come out of the mushrooms, increase the heat again, and sauté for 4–5 minutes, stirring most of the time, until the juices have almost evaporated. Add a squeeze of lemon juice and season to taste with salt and pepper. Stir in the parsley and cook for an additional minute.

3 Transfer the sautéed mushrooms to a warmed serving dish and serve piping hot or warm. Accompany with chunks or slices of crusty bread for mopping up the garlic cooking juices.

deep-fried green chiles

ingredients

**EACH BAG OF CHILES
SERVES 4–6**

olive oil

sweet or hot green chiles

sea salt

method

1 Heat 3 inches/7.5 cm of oil in a heavy-bottom pan until it reaches 375°F/190°C, or until a day-old cube of bread turns brown in 30 seconds.

2 Rinse the chiles and pat them very dry with paper towels. Drop them in the hot oil for no longer than 20 seconds until they turn bright green and the skins blister.

3 Remove with a slotted spoon and drain well on crumpled paper towels. Sprinkle with sea salt and serve at once.

salads & light meals

There are plenty of wonderful ideas here for some rather special light lunch or supper dishes. Salads are always good as they are fairly quick and easy to prepare and can be served, if you like, with some fresh bread to fill up on. An unusual salad combination is Melon, Chorizo, and Artichoke—the glorious color and the cool, sweet taste of the melon contrast really well with the richness of the chorizo. The Tuna and Bean Salad is also excellent—it's especially good made with fresh tuna steak, but for speed you can use canned. The Moorish Zucchini Salad, served on a chunk of bread, is wonderful with its lemon and mint dressing, and the Broiled Bell Pepper Salad is a must—lovely summer sunshine colors for a taste of Spain.

The Spanish version of an omelet, the Tortilla, is irresistible. Don't be alarmed at the amount of oil used to cook the potatoes—it all gets drained off, and it imparts the most delectable flavor. Serve with mixed salad greens for a satisfying outdoor lunch. At its most simple, the tortilla is just eggs, potatoes, and onions, but you can add extras such as spinach or mushrooms for variety.

The Spanish love to mix fish and meat, and this works very well in the tasty little Monkfish, Rosemary, and Bacon skewers. You can use ordinary skewers, but the rosemary stalks are perfect!

a salad of melon, chorizo & artichokes

ingredients

SERVES 8

12 small globe artichokes

juice of $\frac{1}{2}$ lemon

2 tbsp Spanish olive oil

1 small orange-fleshed
melon, such as
cantaloupe

7 oz/200 g chorizo sausage,
outer casing removed

few sprigs of fresh tarragon or
flat-leaf parsley, to garnish

dressing

3 tbsp Spanish extra-virgin
olive oil

1 tbsp red wine vinegar

1 tsp prepared mustard

1 tbsp chopped fresh tarragon

salt and pepper

method

1 To prepare the artichokes, cut off the stalks. With your hands, break off the toughest outer leaves at the base until the tender inside leaves are visible. Using a pair of scissors, cut the spiky tips off the leaves. Using a sharp knife, pare the dark green skin from the base and down the stem. Brush the cut surfaces of the artichokes with lemon juice as you prepare them to prevent discoloration. Unless you are using very young artichokes, use a spoon to remove the choke (the mass of silky hairs). It is very important to remove all the choke as the little barbs, if eaten, can irritate the throat. Cut the artichokes into fourths and brush them again with lemon juice.

2 Heat the olive oil in a large skillet, then add the artichokes and cook, stirring frequently, until the leaves are golden brown. Transfer the artichokes to a serving bowl, and let cool.

3 To prepare the melon, cut in half and scoop out the seeds with a spoon. Cut the flesh into bite-size cubes. Add to the cooled artichokes. Cut the chorizo into bite-size chunks and add to the melon and artichokes.

4 Whisk together the dressing ingredients in a bowl. To serve, toss the salad in the dressing and garnish with tarragon or parsley sprigs.

tuna & bean salad

ingredients

SERVES 4–6

dressing

handful of fresh mint leaves,
    shredded
handful of fresh parsley leaves,
    chopped
1 garlic clove, crushed
4 tbsp extra-virgin olive oil
1 tbsp red wine vinegar
salt and pepper

7 oz/200 g green beans
14 oz/400 g canned small
    white beans, such as
    cannellini, rinsed
    and drained
4 scallions, chopped finely
2 fresh tuna steaks, about
    8 oz/225 g each and
    $^3/_4$ inch/2 cm thick
olive oil, for brushing
9 oz/250 g/2$^1/_4$ cups cherry
    tomatoes, halved
salad greens, to serve
country-style crusty bread,
    to serve
mint and parsley leaves,
    to garnish

method

1 First, make the dressing. Put all the ingredients, with salt and pepper to taste, into a screw-top jar and shake until blended. Pour into a large bowl and set aside.

2 Bring a pan of lightly salted water to a boil. Add the green beans and cook for 3 minutes. Add the white beans and continue cooking for about 4 minutes until the green beans are tender-crisp and the white beans are heated through. Drain well and add to the bowl with the dressing, along with the scallions; toss together.

3 To cook the tuna, heat a ridged grill pan over high heat. Lightly brush the tuna steaks with a little oil on one side, then put them oiled-side down on the grill pan and cook for 2 minutes. Brush the top side with oil, then turn the steak over and continue cooking for 2 minutes for rare or up to 4 minutes for well done.

4 Remove from the grill pan and let the tuna stand for 2 minutes, or until completely cool. When ready to serve, add the tomatoes to the beans and toss lightly. Line a serving platter with salad greens and pile on the bean salad. Flake the tuna over the top. Serve warm or at room temperature with plenty of bread, garnished with the herbs.

salads on bread

ingredients

EACH SALAD QUANTITY
MAKES 12–14 OPEN
SANDWICHES

potato salad

7 oz/200 g new potatoes,
    scrubbed and boiled

1/2 tbsp white wine vinegar

salt and pepper

3–4 tbsp mayonnaise

2 hard-cooked eggs, shelled
    and chopped finely

2 scallions, white and green
    parts chopped finely

12–14 black olives, pitted and
    sliced, to garnish

tuna salad

7 oz/200 g canned tuna in
    olive oil, drained

4 tbsp mayonnaise

2 hard-cooked eggs, shelled
    and chopped finely

1 tomato, broiled and peeled,
    seeded, and chopped
    very finely

2 tsp grated lemon rind

cayenne pepper, to taste

salt and pepper

12–14 anchovy fillets in oil,
    drained, to garnish

24–28 slices from a long, thin
    loaf such as French bread

method

1 Cut the bread on a slight diagonal into slices about 1/4-inch/5-mm thick.

2 To make the potato salad, peel the potatoes as soon as they are cool enough to handle, then cut them into 1/4-inch/5-mm dice. Toss with the vinegar and season with salt and pepper to taste; set aside to cool completely. Stir in the mayonnaise, then fold in the chopped eggs and scallions. Taste and adjust the seasoning. Mound generously on the bread slices, then top each with olive slices.

3 To make the tuna salad, flake the drained tuna into a bowl. Stir in the mayonnaise, then fold in the hard-cooked eggs, tomato, lemon rind, and cayenne. Taste and adjust the seasoning if necessary. Mound generously on the bread slices, then top each with anchovy fillets.

sweet bell peppers stuffed with crab salad

ingredients

MAKES 16

crab salad

8$^1/_2$ oz/240 g crabmeat,
   drained and squeezed dry
1 red bell pepper, broiled,
   peeled, and chopped
about 2 tbsp fresh lemon juice
salt and pepper
7 oz/200 g/scant 1 cup
   cream cheese

16 pimientos del piquillo,
   drained, or freshly roasted
   sweet peppers, tops cut off
chopped fresh parsley,
   to garnish

method

1 First make the crab salad. Pick over the crabmeat and remove any bits of shell. Put half the crabmeat in a food processor with the prepared red bell pepper, 1$^1/2$ tablespoons of the lemon juice, and seasoning to taste. Process until well blended, then transfer to a bowl. Flake and stir in the cream cheese and remaining crabmeat. Taste and add extra lemon juice, if required.

2 Pat dry the pimientos del piquillo and scoop out any seeds that remain in the tips. Use a small spoon to divide the crab salad equally between the sweet peppers, stuffing them generously. Arrange on a large serving dish or individual plates, cover and let chill until required. Just before serving, sprinkle the stuffed peppers with the chopped parsley.

bean & cabrales salad

ingredients

SERVES 4

5¹/₂ oz/150 g/scant 1 cup
   small dried Great Northern
   beans, soaked for 4 hours
   or overnight

1 bay leaf

4 tbsp olive oil

2 tbsp sherry vinegar

2 tsp clear honey

1 tsp Dijon mustard

salt and pepper

2 tbsp toasted slivered almonds

7 oz/200 g Cabrales or other
   bleu cheese, crumbled

method

1 Drain the beans and place in a large, heavy-bottom pan. Pour in enough water to cover, then add the bay leaf and bring to a boil. Boil for 1–1¹/₂ hours, or until tender. Drain, then tip into a bowl and let cool slightly. Remove and discard the bay leaf.

2 Meanwhile, make the dressing. Whisk the olive oil, vinegar, honey, and mustard together in a bowl and season to taste with salt and pepper. Pour the dressing over the beans and toss lightly. Add the almonds and toss lightly again. Let cool to room temperature.

3 To serve, spoon the beans into individual serving bowls and scatter over the cheese.

moorish zucchini salad

ingredients

SERVES 4–6

about 4 tbsp olive oil

1 large garlic clove, halved

18 oz/500 g small zucchini,
    sliced thinly

2 oz/55 g/$\frac{1}{2}$ cup pine nuts

2 oz/55 g/$\frac{1}{3}$ cup raisins

3 tbsp finely chopped mint
    leaves (not spearmint
    or peppermint)

about 2 tbsp lemon juice,
    or to taste

salt and pepper

method

1 Heat the oil in a large skillet over medium heat. Add the garlic and let it cook until golden to flavor the oil, then remove and discard. Add the zucchini and cook, stirring until just tender. Immediately remove from the skillet and transfer to a large serving bowl.

2 Add the pine nuts, raisins, mint, lemon juice, and salt and pepper to taste and stir together. Taste, and add more oil, lemon juice and seasoning, if necessary.

3 Set aside and let cool completely. Cover and let chill for at least 3$\frac{1}{2}$ hours. Remove from the fridge 10 minutes before serving.

broiled bell pepper salad

ingredients

SERVES 4–6

6 large red, orange, or yellow
    bell peppers, each cut in
    half lengthwise, broiled,
    and peeled
4 hard-cooked eggs, shelled
12 anchovy fillets in oil, drained
12 large black olives
extra-virgin olive oil or
    garlic-flavored olive oil
sherry vinegar
salt and pepper
country-style crusty bread,
    to serve

method

1 Remove any cores and seeds from the broiled bell peppers and cut into thin strips. Arrange on a large serving platter.

2 Cut the eggs into wedges and arrange over the bell pepper strips, along with the anchovy fillets and olives.

3 Drizzle oil over the top, then splash with sherry vinegar, adding both to taste. Sprinkle a little salt and pepper over the top and serve with bread.

beef skewers with orange & garlic

ingredients

SERVES 6–8

3 tbsp white wine

2 tbsp olive oil

3 garlic cloves, finely chopped

juice of 1 orange

1 lb/450 g rump steak, cubed

1 lb/450 g baby onions, halved

2 orange bell peppers, seeded
   and cut into squares

8 oz/225 g cherry tomatoes,
   halved

salt and pepper

method

1 Mix the wine, olive oil, garlic, and orange juice together in a shallow, nonmetallic dish. Add the cubes of steak, season to taste with salt and pepper, and toss to coat. Cover with plastic wrap and let marinate in the refrigerator for 2–8 hours.

2 Preheat the broiler to high. Drain the steak, reserving the marinade. Thread the steak, onions, bell peppers, and tomatoes alternately onto several small skewers.

3 Cook the skewers under the hot broiler, turning and brushing frequently with the marinade, for 10 minutes, or until cooked through. Transfer to warmed serving plates and serve immediately.

miniature pork brochettes

ingredients

MAKES 12

1 lb/450 g lean boneless pork
3 tbsp Spanish olive oil, plus
    extra for oiling (optional)
grated rind and juice of
    1 large lemon
2 garlic cloves, crushed
2 tbsp chopped fresh
    flat-leaf parsley, plus extra
    to garnish
1 tbsp ras-el-hanout
    spice blend
salt and pepper

method

1 Cut the pork into pieces about 3/4 inch/2 cm square and put in a large, shallow, nonmetallic dish that will hold the pieces in a single layer.

2 To prepare the marinade, put all the remaining ingredients in a bowl and mix well together. Pour the marinade over the pork and toss the meat in it until well coated. Cover the dish and let marinate in the refrigerator overnight, stirring the pork 2–3 times.

3 You can use wooden or metal skewers to cook the brochettes and for this recipe you will need about 12 x 6-inch/15-cm skewers. If you are using wooden ones, soak them in cold water for about 30 minutes prior to using. This helps to stop them burning and the food sticking to them during cooking. Metal skewers simply need to be greased, and flat ones should be used in preference to round ones to prevent the food on them falling off.

4 Preheat the broiler, grill pan, or barbecue. Thread 3 marinated pork pieces, leaving a little space between each piece, onto each prepared skewer. Cook the brochettes for 10–15 minutes, or until tender and lightly charred, turning several times and basting with the remaining marinade during cooking. Serve the pork brochettes piping hot, garnished with parsley.

fava beans with ham

ingredients

SERVES 4–6

8 oz/225 g/scant $^{1}/_{2}$ cup
   fresh or frozen shelled
   fava beans
2 tbsp extra-virgin olive oil
1 Spanish red onion,
   chopped very finely
1 slice medium-thick serrano
   ham or prosciutto, chopped
fresh parsley, chopped finely,
   to taste
salt and pepper
French bread, to serve

method

1 Bring a large pan of salted water to a boil. Add the beans and continue to boil for 5–10 minutes until just tender. Drain and put in a bowl of cold water to stop further cooking. Unless the beans are young and tiny, peel off the outer skins.

2 Meanwhile, heat 1 tablespoon of the oil in a skillet over medium-high heat. Add the onion and cook for about 5 minutes until soft, but not brown. Add the beans.

3 Stir in the ham and parsley and check the seasoning; the meat is salty, so don't add salt until after tasting. Transfer to a serving bowl and drizzle with the remaining oil. Serve at room temperature with slices of French bread.

chickpeas & chorizo

ingredients

SERVES 4–6

4 tbsp olive oil

1 onion, chopped finely

1 large garlic clove, crushed

9 oz/250 g chorizo sausage in
  one piece, casing removed
  and cut into $^1/_2$-inch/
  1-cm dice

14 oz/400 g canned chickpeas,
  drained and rinsed

6 pimientos del piquillo,
  drained, patted dry,
  and sliced

1 tbsp sherry vinegar,
  or to taste

salt and pepper

finely chopped fresh parsley,
  to garnish

crusty bread slices, to serve

method

1 Heat the oil in a large, heavy-bottom skillet over medium heat. Add the onion and garlic and cook, stirring occasionally, until the onion is softened, but not browned. Stir in the chorizo and continue cooking until it is heated through.

2 Tip the mixture into a bowl and stir in the chickpeas and peppers. Splash with sherry vinegar and season with salt and pepper to taste. Serve hot or at room temperature, generously sprinkled with parsley, with plenty of crusty bread.

chorizo pizza

ingredients

SERVES 4–6

6 tomatoes, sliced

2 onions, finely chopped

12 black olives

4 serrano ham slices

10 ready-to-eat chorizo
    sausage slices

2 tbsp chopped mixed
    fresh herbs

2 oz/55 g Tronchon or
    mozzarella cheese,
    thinly sliced

2 fl oz/50 ml/$\frac{1}{4}$ cup olive oil

salt and pepper

pizza base

$\frac{3}{4}$ oz/20 g/1 package
    fresh yeast

9 oz/250 g/1$\frac{2}{3}$ cups all-
    purpose flour, plus extra
    for dusting

8 fl oz/225 ml/1 cup
    lukewarm water

pinch of salt

2 fl oz/50 ml/$\frac{1}{4}$ cup olive oil

method

1 First make the pizza base. Mix the yeast with $\frac{1}{3}$ cup of the flour and the water in a bowl. Let stand for 10 minutes.

2 Meanwhile, sift the remaining flour with the salt into a large bowl and make a well in the center. Add the yeast mixture and the olive oil. Using an electric mixer, mix well for 5–10 minutes. Cover with a clean tea towel and let stand in a warm place until the dough has doubled in size.

3 Preheat the oven to 425°F/220°C and place a baking sheet in the oven to warm. Pat out the pizza dough into a 11–12-inch/28–30-cm circle on a lightly floured counter and make a slightly raised rim around the edge.

4 Arrange the tomato slices on top of the pizza dough and season to taste with salt, then cover with the onion. Add the olives, ham, and chorizo, then season to taste with pepper and sprinkle over the herbs. Top with the cheese slices and drizzle with the olive oil.

5 Carefully transfer the pizza to the preheated baking sheet and bake in the preheated oven for 30 minutes, or until the cheese has melted and is bubbling and the rim has lightly browned. Cut into wedges and serve.

chicken livers in sherry sauce

ingredients

SERVES 6

1 lb/450 g chicken livers

2 tbsp Spanish olive oil

1 small onion, finely chopped

2 garlic cloves, finely chopped

3 1/2 fl oz/100 ml/generous
   1/3 cup dry Spanish sherry

salt and pepper

2 tbsp chopped fresh
   flat-leaf parsley

crusty bread or toast, to serve

method

1 If necessary, trim the chicken livers, cutting away any ducts and gristle, then cut them into small, bite-size pieces.

2 Heat the olive oil in a large, heavy-bottom skillet. Add the onion and cook for 5 minutes, or until softened but not browned. Add the garlic and cook for an additional 30 seconds.

3 Add the chicken livers to the skillet and cook for 2–3 minutes, stirring all the time, until they are firm and have changed color on the outside but are still pink and soft in the center. Using a slotted spoon, lift the chicken livers from the pan, transfer them to a large, warmed serving dish or several smaller ones, and keep warm.

4 Add the sherry to the skillet, increase the heat, and let it bubble for 3–4 minutes to evaporate the alcohol and reduce slightly. At the same time, deglaze the skillet by scraping and stirring all the bits on the bottom of the skillet into the sauce with a wooden spoon. Season to taste with salt and pepper.

5 Pour the sherry sauce over the chicken livers and sprinkle over the parsley. Serve piping hot, accompanied by chunks or slices of crusty bread or toast to mop up the sherry sauce.

crispy chicken & ham croquettes

ingredients

MAKES 8

4 tbsp olive oil

4 tbsp all-purpose flour

7 fl oz/200 ml/scant
    1 cup milk

4 oz/115 g cooked chicken,
    ground

2 oz/55 g serrano or cooked
    ham, very finely chopped

1 tbsp chopped fresh
    flat-leaf parsley, plus extra
    sprigs to garnish

small pinch of freshly
    grated nutmeg

salt and pepper

1 egg, beaten

2 oz/55 g/1 cup day-old white
    bread crumbs

corn oil, for deep-frying

aïoli, to serve (see page 44)

method

1 Heat the olive oil in a pan. Stir in the flour to form a paste and cook gently for 1 minute, stirring constantly. Gradually stir in the milk until smooth and slowly bring to a boil, stirring, until the mixture boils and thickens.

2 Remove from the heat, add the ground chicken, and beat until the mixture is smooth. Add the chopped ham, parsley, and nutmeg and mix well together. Season to taste with salt and pepper. Put in a dish and let stand for 30 minutes, until cool, then cover and let rest in the refrigerator for 2–3 hours or overnight.

3 Pour the beaten egg onto a plate and spread out the bread crumbs on a separate plate. Divide the chilled chicken mixture into 8 portions and form each into a cylindrical shape. Dip the croquettes, one at a time, in the beaten egg, then roll in the bread crumbs to coat. Let chill in the refrigerator for 1 hour.

4 Heat the oil in a deep-fryer to 350–375°F/ 180–190°C. Add the croquettes, in batches to prevent the temperature of the oil dropping, and deep-fry for 5–10 minutes, or until golden brown and crispy. Remove with a slotted spoon and drain well on paper towels.

5 Serve the croquettes piping hot, garnished with parsley sprigs, with a bowl of aïoli.

traditional catalan salt cod salad

ingredients

SERVES 4–6

14 oz/400 g dried salt cod in one piece

6 scallions, sliced thinly on the diagonal

6 tbsp extra-virgin olive oil

1 tbsp sherry vinegar

1 tbsp lemon juice

pepper

2 large red bell peppers, broiled, peeled, seeded, and diced very finely

12 large black olives, pitted and sliced

2 large, juicy tomatoes, sliced thinly, to serve

2 tbsp very finely chopped fresh parsley, to garnish

method

1 Place the dried salt cod in a large bowl, cover with cold water, and let soak for at least 48 hours, changing the water occasionally.

2 Pat the salt cod very dry with paper towels and remove the skin and bones, then use your fingers to tear into fine shreds. Put in a large, nonmetallic bowl with the scallions, oil, vinegar, and lemon juice, and toss together. Season with freshly ground black pepper, cover, and put in the refrigerator to marinate for 3 hours.

3 Stir in the bell peppers and olives. Taste and adjust the seasoning, if necessary, remembering that the cod and olives might be salty. Arrange the tomato slices on a large platter or individual plates and spoon the salad on top. Sprinkle with parsley and serve.

monkfish, rosemary & bacon skewers

ingredients

MAKES 12

9 oz/250 g monkfish fillet
12 stalks of fresh rosemary
3 tbsp Spanish olive oil
juice of $1/2$ small lemon
1 garlic clove, crushed
salt and pepper
6 thick slices Canadian bacon
lemon wedges, to garnish
aïoli, to serve (see page 44)

method

1 Slice the monkfish fillets in half lengthwise, then cut each fillet into 12 bite-size chunks to make a total of 24 pieces. Put the monkfish pieces in a large bowl.

2 To prepare the rosemary skewers, strip the leaves off the stalks and set them aside, leaving a few leaves at one end.

3 For the marinade, finely chop the reserved leaves and whisk together in a bowl with the olive oil, lemon juice, garlic, and salt and pepper to taste. Add the monkfish pieces and toss until coated in the marinade. Cover and let marinate in the refrigerator for 1–2 hours.

4 Cut each bacon slice in half lengthwise, then in half widthwise, and roll up each piece. Thread 2 pieces of monkfish alternately with 2 bacon rolls onto the rosemary skewers.

5 Preheat the broiler, grill pan, or barbecue. If you are cooking the skewers under a broiler, arrange them on the broiler pan so that the leaves of the rosemary skewers protrude from the broiler and do not catch fire. Broil the monkfish and bacon skewers for 10 minutes, turning from time to time and basting with any remaining marinade, or until cooked. Serve hot, garnished with lemon wedges, with a bowl of aïoli.

fresh salmon in mojo sauce

ingredients

SERVES 8

4 fresh salmon fillets, weighing
    about 1 lb 10 oz/750 g
    in total
salt and pepper
3 tbsp Spanish olive oil
1 fresh flat-leaf parsley sprig,
    to garnish

mojo sauce

2 garlic cloves, peeled
2 tsp paprika
1 tsp ground cumin
5 tbsp Spanish extra-virgin
    olive oil
2 tbsp white wine vinegar
salt

method

1 To prepare the mojo sauce, put the garlic, paprika, and cumin in the bowl of a food processor and, using a pulsing action, blend for 1 minute to mix well together. With the motor still running, add 1 tablespoon of the olive oil, drop by drop, through the feeder tube. When it has been added, scrape down the sides of the bowl with a spatula, then very slowly continue to pour in the oil in a thin, steady stream, until all the oil has been added and the sauce has slightly thickened. Add the vinegar and blend for an additional 1 minute. Season the sauce with salt to taste.

2 To prepare the salmon, remove the skin, cut each fillet in half widthwise, then cut lengthwise into 3/4-inch/2-cm thick slices, discarding any bones. Season the pieces of fish to taste with salt and pepper.

3 Heat the olive oil in a large, heavy-bottom skillet. When hot, add the pieces of fish and cook for about 10 minutes, depending on their thickness, turning occasionally until cooked and browned on both sides.

4 Transfer the salmon to a warmed serving dish, drizzle over some of the mojo sauce, and serve hot, garnished with parsley, and accompanied by the remaining sauce.

fava beans with cheese & shrimp

ingredients

SERVES 6

1 lb 2 oz/500 g shelled fresh
    or frozen fava beans

2 fresh thyme sprigs

8 oz/225 g cooked
    shelled shrimp

8 oz/225 g Queso Majorero or
    Gruyère cheese, diced

6 tbsp olive oil

2 tbsp lemon juice

1 garlic clove, finely chopped

salt and pepper

method

1 Bring a large pan of lightly salted water to a boil. Add the fava beans and 1 thyme sprig, then reduce the heat and simmer, covered, for 7 minutes. Drain well, refresh under cold running water, then drain again.

2 Unless the fava beans are very young, remove and discard the outer skins. Place the beans in a bowl and add the shrimp and cheese.

3 Chop the remaining thyme sprig. Whisk the olive oil, lemon juice, garlic, and chopped thyme together in a separate bowl and season to taste with salt and pepper.

4 Pour the dressing over the bean mixture. Toss lightly and serve.

scallops in saffron sauce

ingredients

SERVES 8

5 fl oz/150 ml/^{2}/$_3$ cup dry
    white wine

5 fl oz/150 ml/^{2}/$_3$ cup
    fish stock

large pinch of saffron threads

2 lb/900 g shelled scallops,
    preferably large ones,
    with corals

salt and pepper

3 tbsp Spanish olive oil

1 small onion, finely chopped

2 garlic cloves, finely chopped

5 fl oz/150 ml/^{2}/$_3$ cup heavy
    cream

squeeze of lemon juice

chopped fresh flat-leaf
    parsley, to garnish

crusty bread, to serve

method

1 Put the wine, fish stock, and saffron in a pan and bring to a boil. Lower the heat, cover, and let simmer gently for 15 minutes.

2 Meanwhile, remove and discard from each scallop the tough, white muscle that is found opposite the coral, and separate the coral from the scallop. Slice the scallops and corals vertically into thick slices. Dry well on paper towels, then season to taste.

3 Heat the olive oil in a large, heavy-bottom skillet. Add the onion and garlic and cook until softened and lightly browned. Add the sliced scallops to the skillet and cook gently for 5 minutes, stirring occasionally, or until they turn just opaque. Overcooking the scallops will make them tough and rubbery.

4 Using a slotted spoon, remove the scallops from the skillet and transfer to a warmed plate. Add the saffron liquid to the skillet, bring to a boil, and boil rapidly until reduced to about half. Lower the heat and gradually stir in the cream, just a little at a time. Let simmer gently until the sauce thickens.

5 Return the scallops to the skillet and let simmer for 1–2 minutes just to heat through. Add a squeeze of lemon juice and season to taste with salt and pepper. Serve the scallops hot, garnished with the parsley, with slices or chunks of crusty bread.

seared scallops

ingredients

SERVES 4–6

4 tbsp olive oil

3 tbsp orange juice

2 tsp hazelnut oil

24 shelled scallops

salad greens (optional)

6 oz/175 g Cabrales or other
    bleu cheese, crumbled

2 tbsp chopped fresh dill

salt and pepper

method

1 Whisk 3 tablespoons of the olive oil, the orange juice, and hazelnut oil together in a pitcher and season to taste with salt and pepper.

2 Heat the remaining olive oil in a large, heavy-bottom skillet. Add the scallops and cook over high heat for 1 minute on each side, or until golden.

3 Transfer the scallops to a bed of salad greens or individual plates. Scatter over the cheese and dill, then drizzle with the dressing. Serve warm.

tortilla espanola

ingredients

SERVES 8

1 lb/450 g waxy potatoes,
    peeled and cut into
    small cubes and dried
    well on a dish towel
4 fl oz/600 g/scant 2 cups
    Spanish olive oil
2 onions, chopped
2 large eggs
salt and pepper
sprigs of fresh flat-leaf
    parsley, to garnish

method

1 Heat the olive oil in a large, heavy-bottom skillet. Add the potato cubes and onions, then lower the heat and cook, stirring frequently so that the potatoes do not clump together, for 20 minutes, or until tender but not browned. Place a strainer over a large bowl and drain the potatoes and onions well. Set aside the oil.

2 Beat the eggs lightly in a large bowl and season well with salt and pepper. Gently stir in the potatoes and onions.

3 Wipe out the skillet with paper towels and heat 2 tablespoons of the reserved olive oil. When hot, add the egg and potato mixture, lower the heat and cook for 3–5 minutes, or until the underside is just set. Use a spatula to submerge the potatoes down into the egg and loosen the tortilla from the bottom of the skillet to stop it sticking.

4 Cover the tortilla with a plate, and hold the plate in place with the other hand. Drain off the oil in the skillet, then quickly invert the tortilla onto the plate. Return the skillet to the heat and add a little more oil if necessary. Slide the tortilla, cooked side uppermost, back into the skillet and cook for an additional 3–5 minutes, or until set underneath.

5 Slide the tortilla onto a serving plate and let stand for about 15 minutes. Serve warm or cold, garnished with parsley sprigs.

basque scrambled eggs

ingredients

SERVES 4–6

olive oil

1 large onion, chopped finely

1 large red bell pepper, cored, seeded, and chopped

1 large green bell pepper, cored, seeded, and chopped

2 large tomatoes, peeled, seeded, and chopped

2 oz/55 g chorizo sausage, sliced thinly, casings removed, if preferred

3 tbsp butter

10 large eggs, beaten lightly

salt and pepper

4–6 thick slices country-style bread, toasted, to serve

method

1 Heat 2 tablespoons of oil in a large, heavy-bottom skillet over medium-high heat. Add the onion and bell peppers and cook for about 5 minutes, or until the vegetables are soft, but not brown. Add the tomatoes and heat through. Transfer to a plate and keep warm in a preheated low oven.

2 Add another tablespoon of oil to the skillet. Add the chorizo and cook for 30 seconds, just to warm through and flavor the oil. Add the sausage to the reserved vegetables.

3 There should be about 2 tablespoons of oil in the skillet, so add a little extra, if necessary, to make up the amount. Add the butter and let melt. Season the eggs with salt and pepper, then add them to the skillet. Scramble the eggs until they are cooked to the desired degree of firmness. Add extra seasoning to taste. Return the vegetables to the skillet and stir through. Serve at once with hot toast.

spinach & mushroom tortilla

ingredients

SERVES 4

2 tbsp olive oil

3 shallots, finely chopped

12 oz/350 g mushrooms, sliced

10 oz/280 g fresh spinach
   leaves, coarse stems
   removed

2 oz/55 g/$\frac{1}{2}$ cup toasted
   slivered almonds

5 eggs

2 tbsp chopped fresh parsley

2 tbsp cold water

3 oz/85 g mature Mahon,
   Manchego, or Parmesan
   cheese, grated

salt and pepper

method

1 Heat the olive oil in a skillet that can safely be placed under the broiler. Add the shallots and cook over low heat, stirring occasionally, for 5 minutes, or until softened. Add the mushrooms and cook, stirring frequently, for an additional 4 minutes. Add the spinach, then increase the heat to medium and cook, stirring frequently, for 3–4 minutes, or until wilted. Reduce the heat, then season to taste with salt and pepper and stir in the slivered almonds.

2 Beat the eggs with the parsley, water, and salt and pepper to taste in a bowl. Pour the mixture into the skillet and cook for 5–8 minutes, or until the underside is set. Lift the edge of the tortilla occasionally to let the uncooked egg run underneath. Meanwhile, preheat the broiler to high.

3 Sprinkle the grated cheese over the tortilla and cook under the preheated hot broiler for 3 minutes, or until the top is set and the cheese has melted. Serve, lukewarm or cold, cut into thin wedges.

paella-stuffed mediterranean bell peppers

ingredients

SERVES 4

$1/2$ tsp saffron threads

2 tbsp hot water

3 tbsp olive oil

1 zucchini, diced

$5^1/2$ oz/150 g white mushrooms

2 scallions, diced

2 garlic cloves, crushed

1 tsp paprika

$1/4$ tsp cayenne pepper

9 oz/250 g canned red kidney
   beans (drained weight)

8 oz/225 g tomatoes,
   peeled and chopped

13 oz/375 g/generous
   $1^1/2$ cups medium-grain
   paella rice

2 pints/1.2 liters/$5^1/2$ cups
   simmering vegetable stock

4 oz/125 g/scant $1/2$ cup peas

1 tbsp chopped fresh flat-leaf
   parsley, plus extra
   to garnish

4 large red bell peppers, tops
   cut off and set aside and
   seeds removed

$3^1/2$ oz/100 g Manchego or
   Parmesan cheese, grated

salt and pepper

mixed salad, to serve

method

1 Put the saffron threads and water in a bowl and let infuse. Meanwhile, heat the oil in a paella pan over medium heat and cook the zucchini, stirring, for 3 minutes. Add the mushrooms and scallions and cook, stirring, until softened. Add the garlic, paprika, cayenne pepper, and saffron and its soaking liquid and cook, stirring, for 1 minute. Add the beans and tomatoes and cook, stirring, for 2 minutes.

2 Add the rice and cook, stirring, for 1 minute to coat. Add most of the stock and bring to a boil, then let simmer, uncovered, for 10 minutes. Do not stir during cooking, but shake the pan once or twice. Add the peas and parsley, season to taste, and shake the pan. Cook for 10–15 minutes, or until the rice grains are cooked. When all the liquid has been absorbed, remove from the heat. Cover with foil and let stand for 5 minutes.

3 Blanch the red bell peppers and their tops in a pan of boiling water for 2 minutes. Drain and pat dry with paper towels. Spoon a little cheese into each, then fill with paella and top with the remaining cheese. Replace the tops. Wrap each bell pepper in foil, then stand in an ovenproof dish and bake in a preheated oven, 350°F/180°C, for 25–30 minutes. Garnish with parsley and serve with salad and bread.

main meals

Think of Spain and you tend to think of sunshine and heat, but the weather isn't always wonderful and some of the best-loved dishes are hearty, richly flavored stews intended to keep the chill of a cold winter at bay—Lamb Stew with Chickpeas, for example, is satisfying, warming, and delicious. The Spanish are great meat-eaters, and vegetables are served as an integral part of the main course, rather than on the side. If you thought you didn't like fava beans, try them, young and tiny if possible, otherwise popped out of their tough gray skins, in a stew with chicken and mushrooms and you will almost certainly be converted.

The miles of coastal waters that surround much of Spain mean that fish and seafood make regular appearances in the Spanish kitchen. Fish stews are made using the catch of the day, but some ingredients remain the same—a Catalan Fish Stew will always feature saffron, almonds, garlic, and tomatoes. Fish is often cooked quite simply, roasted or pan-fried, and served with a sauce or, in Catalonia, on a bed of spinach with pine nuts, raisins, and garlic.

Fish and meat are often combined in what has come to be considered the national dish of Spain—paella. For lovers of this wonderful invention, we've included several recipes!

meatballs with peas

ingredients

SERVES 4–6

1 lb 2 oz/500 g/2$\frac{1}{4}$ cups
   lean ground beef

1 onion, grated

2 oz/55g/1 cup fresh white
   bread crumbs

1 egg, beaten lightly

2 tbsp fresh parsley,
   chopped finely

salt and pepper

olive oil

2 large onions, sliced thinly

7 oz/200 g/1$\frac{1}{2}$ cups
   frozen peas

tomato and bell pepper sauce

4 tbsp olive oil

10 large garlic cloves

5 oz/140 g shallots, chopped

4 large red bell peppers,
   cored, seeded, and
   chopped

2 lb 4 oz/1 kg good-flavored
   ripe, fresh tomatoes,
   chopped

2 thin strips freshly pared
   orange rind

salt and pepper

method

1 To make the tomato and bell pepper sauce, heat the oil in a large pan over medium heat. Add the garlic, shallots, and bell peppers and cook for 10 minutes, stirring occasionally, until the bell peppers are soft, but not brown. Add the tomatoes and orange rind, season to taste and bring to a boil. Let simmer, uncovered, over low heat for 45 minutes, or until the sauce thickens. Purée in a food processor, then press through a fine strainer.

2 Put the meat in a bowl with the grated onion, bread crumbs, egg, parsley, and salt and pepper to taste. Squeeze all the ingredients together. With wet hands, shape the mixture into 12 balls. Let chill for at least 20 minutes.

3 Heat a little of the oil in a large skillet. Cook the meatballs, in batches, in a single layer, for about 5 minutes until brown, adding more oil if necessary. Remove and set aside. Pour all but 2 tablespoons of oil from the skillet. Add the onions and cook until soft, but not brown.

4 Return the meatballs to the skillet. Stir in the tomato and bell pepper sauce and bring to a boil, gently spooning the sauce and onions over the meatballs. Reduce the heat, cover, and let simmer for 20 minutes. Add the peas and simmer for 7–10 minutes until the peas are tender and the meatballs cooked through. Serve at once.

veal with pickled vegetables

ingredients

SERVES 4

vegetable escabeche

5 fl oz/150 ml/$2/3$ cup olive oil

4 shallots, sliced

2 pinches of saffron threads

1 lb/450 g young carrots, peeled and sliced thinly

8 oz/225 g green beans, chopped small

8 oz/225 g tiny cauliflower florets

3 tbsp white wine vinegar

1 tsp coriander seeds, crushed

$1/2$ tsp black peppercorns, crushed

1 bay leaf, torn in half

4 veal loin chops, about 8 oz/225 g each and $3/4$ inch/2 cm thick

salt and pepper

2 tbsp finely chopped fresh chives, to garnish

garlic-flavored olive oil, for drizzling

method

1 To make the vegetable escabeche, heat the oil in a skillet over medium heat. Add the shallots and saffron and cook for 5–7 minutes until the shallots start to caramelize. Add the carrots, beans, and cauliflower. Reduce the heat to very low, cover, and cook for 5–8 minutes until the vegetables are tender-crisp. Stir in the vinegar, coriander seeds, peppercorns, and bay leaf. Remove from the heat and let cool, unless you are serving the dish immediately.

2 When ready to cook, lightly drizzle the chops with more oil and season with salt and pepper to taste. Place under a preheated hot broiler, about 4 inches/10 cm from the source of the heat, and broil for 3 minutes. Turn the chops over and broil for an additional 2 minutes if you like them cooked medium.

3 Transfer the chops to individual plates and spoon a little of the escabeche on the side of each. Sprinkle the vegetables with the chives, and drizzle with a little of the flavored oil. Serve at once.

paella with pork & charbroiled bell peppers

ingredients

SERVES 4–6

6 tbsp olive oil

3 tbsp sherry vinegar

1/4 tsp cayenne pepper

1 tsp paprika

6 oz/175 g pork tenderloin

1/2 tsp saffron threads

2 tbsp hot water

6 oz/175 g Spanish chorizo
sausage, casing removed,
cut into 1/2-inch/1-cm slices

1 large onion, chopped

2 garlic cloves, crushed

8 oz/225 g tomatoes, peeled
and cut into wedges

13 oz/375 g/generous
1 1/2 cups medium-grain
paella rice

1 tbsp chopped fresh thyme

3 1/2 fl oz/100 ml/generous
1/3 cup white wine

2 pints/1.2 liters/5 cups
simmering chicken stock

salt and pepper

2 large red bell peppers,
seeded, broiled, peeled,
and cut into long strips,
1/2 inch/1 cm wide

1 lemon, cut into wedges,
to serve

method

1 Mix half the oil, vinegar, cayenne pepper, and paprika in a shallow nonmetallic dish. Season the pork to taste on both sides, then coat it in the oil mixture. Cover with plastic wrap and let marinate in the refrigerator for 2 hours, then remove and cut into bite-size chunks.

2 Put the saffron threads and water in a bowl and let infuse. Heat the remaining oil in a paella pan and cook the pork and marinade over medium heat, stirring, for 5 minutes. Add the chorizo and onion and cook, stirring, to soften the onion. Add the garlic and saffron and its soaking liquid and cook, stirring, for 1 minute. Add the tomatoes and cook, stirring, for 2 minutes. Add the rice and thyme and cook, stirring, for 1 minute to coat the rice.

3 Add the wine and most of the stock and bring to a boil, then let simmer, uncovered, for 10 minutes. Do not stir during cooking, but shake the pan once or twice. Season to taste, cook for 10–15 minutes, or until the rice is almost cooked. Add the charbroiled bell peppers and a little extra stock if necessary, then shake the pan. When all the liquid has been absorbed and you detect a faint toasty aroma coming from the rice, remove from the heat. Cover the pan with foil and let stand for 5 minutes. Serve with the lemon wedges.

chorizo & ham paella

ingredients

SERVES 4–6

$1/2$ tsp saffron threads

2 tbsp hot water

3 tbsp olive oil

6 oz/175 g Spanish chorizo
   sausage, casing removed,
   cut into $1/2$-inch/1-cm slices

6 oz/175 g serrano ham, diced
   (if unavailable, use
   prosciutto)

1 large onion, chopped

2 garlic cloves, crushed

1 tsp paprika

$1/4$ tsp cayenne pepper

8 oz/225 g tomatoes, peeled
   and cut into wedges

1 red bell pepper, halved
   and seeded, then broiled,
   peeled, and sliced

12 oz/350 g/generous
   $1 1/2$ cups medium-grain
   paella rice

1 tbsp chopped fresh thyme

3 fl oz/125 ml/generous
   $1/3$ cup white wine

2 pints/1.2 liters/5 cups
   simmering chicken stock

salt and pepper

1 tbsp chopped fresh parsley,
   to garnish

1 lemon, cut into wedges,
   to serve

method

1 Put the saffron threads and water in a small bowl and let infuse for a few minutes.

2 Heat 2 tablespoons of the oil in a paella pan and cook the chorizo and ham over medium heat, stirring, for 5 minutes. Transfer to a bowl and set aside. Heat the remaining oil in the pan and cook the onion, stirring, until softened. Add the garlic, paprika, cayenne pepper, and saffron and its soaking liquid and cook, stirring constantly, for 1 minute. Add the tomato wedges and red bell pepper slices and cook, stirring, for an additional 2 minutes.

3 Add the rice and thyme and cook, stirring, for 1 minute to coat the rice. Pour in the wine and most of the hot stock and bring to a boil, then let simmer, uncovered, for 10 minutes. Do not stir during cooking, but shake the pan once or twice and when adding ingredients. Season to taste and cook for 10 minutes, or until the rice is almost cooked. If the liquid is absorbed too quickly, pour in a little more hot stock. Return the chorizo and ham and any accumulated juices to the pan. Cook for 2 minutes.

4 When all the liquid has been absorbed and you detect a faint toasty aroma coming from the rice, remove from the heat. Cover the pan with foil and let stand for 5 minutes. Garnish with parsley and serve with lemon wedges.

sausages with lentils

ingredients

SERVES 4–6

2 tbsp olive oil

12 merguez sausages

2 onions, chopped finely

2 red bell peppers, cored, seeded, and chopped

1 orange or yellow bell pepper, cored, seeded, and chopped

10 oz/280 g/scant 1¹/₂ cups small green lentils, rinsed

1 tsp dried thyme or marjoram

16 fl oz/450 ml/2 cups vegetable stock

salt and pepper

4 tbsp chopped fresh parsley

red wine vinegar, to serve

method

1 Heat the oil in a large, preferably nonstick, lidded skillet over medium-high heat. Add the sausages and cook, stirring frequently, for about 10 minutes until they are brown all over and cooked through; remove from the skillet and set aside.

2 Pour off all but 2 tablespoons of oil from the skillet. Add the onions and bell peppers and cook for about 5 minutes until soft, but not brown. Add the lentils and thyme or marjoram and stir until coated with oil.

3 Stir in the stock and bring to a boil. Reduce the heat, cover, and let simmer for about 30 minutes until the lentils are tender and the liquid is absorbed; if the lentils are tender, but too much liquid remains, uncover the skillet and let simmer until it evaporates. Season to taste with salt and pepper.

4 Return the sausages to the skillet and reheat. Stir in the parsley. Serve the sausages with lentils on the side, then splash a little red wine vinegar over each portion.

fiery chile & chorizo paella

ingredients

SERVES 4–6

$^1/_2$ tsp saffron threads

2 tbsp hot water

$5^1/_2$ oz/150 g pork tenderloin,
    cut into bite-size chunks

$5^1/_2$ oz/150 g chicken breast,
    cut into bite-size chunks

1 tsp paprika

$^1/_2$ tsp cayenne pepper

3 tbsp olive oil

$5^1/_2$ oz/150 g Spanish chorizo
    sausage, casing removed,
    cut into $^1/_2$-inch/1-cm slices

1 large red onion, chopped

2 garlic cloves, crushed

1 small fresh red chile,
    seeded and minced

8 oz/225 g cherry tomatoes,

1 red bell pepper

1 green bell pepper

13 oz/375 g/generous
    $1^1/_2$ cups medium-grain
    paella rice

1 tbsp chopped fresh thyme,
    plus extra sprigs to garnish

2 tbsp sherry

$3^1/_2$ fl oz/100 ml/generous
    $^1/_3$ cup white wine

2 pints/1.2 liters/5 cups
    simmering chicken stock

12 pitted black olives, halved

salt and pepper

method

1 Put the saffron threads and water in a small bowl and let infuse for a few minutes. Season the pork and chicken with paprika, cayenne pepper, salt, and pepper. Cut the tomatoes in half. Broil, peel, and chop the bell peppers.

2 Heat the oil in a paella pan and cook the pork, chicken, and chorizo over medium heat, stirring, for 5 minutes. Add the onion and cook, stirring, until softened. Add the garlic, chile, and saffron and its soaking liquid and cook, stirring constantly, for 1 minute. Add the tomatoes and bell peppers and cook, stirring, for an additional 2 minutes.

3 Add the rice and thyme and cook, stirring, for 1 minute, to coat the rice. Add the sherry, wine, and most of the hot stock and bring to a boil, then let simmer, uncovered, for 10 minutes. Do not stir during cooking, but shake the pan once or twice. Add the olives and season to taste. Shake the pan and cook for 10 minutes, until the rice is almost cooked. Add a little more stock if necessary, then shake the pan. Taste and adjust the seasoning and cook for an additional 2 minutes.

4 When all the liquid has been absorbed and you detect a faint toasty aroma coming from the rice, remove from the heat. Cover with foil and let stand for 5 minutes. Garnish with thyme sprigs and serve with lemon wedges.

lamb stew with chickpeas

ingredients

SERVES 4–6

olive oil

8 oz/225 g chorizo sausage,
   cut into ¼-inch/5-mm
   thick slices, casings
   removed

2 large onions, chopped

6 large garlic cloves, crushed

2 lb/900 g boned leg of lamb,
   cut into 2-inch/5-cm chunks

9 fl oz/250 ml/scant 1¼ cups
   lamb stock or water

4 fl oz/125 ml/½ cup red
   wine, such as Rioja or
   Tempranillo

2 tbsp sherry vinegar

1 lb 12 oz/800 g canned
   chopped tomatoes

salt and pepper

4 sprigs fresh thyme

2 bay leaves

½ tsp sweet Spanish paprika

1 lb 12 oz/800 g canned
   chickpeas, rinsed and
   drained

sprigs fresh thyme, to garnish

method

1 Heat 4 tablespoons of oil in a large, heavy-bottom casserole over medium-high heat. Reduce the heat, add the chorizo, and cook for 1 minute; set aside. Add the onions to the casserole and cook for 2 minutes, then add the garlic and continue cooking for 3 minutes, or until the onions are soft, but not brown. Remove from the casserole and set aside.

2 Heat an additional 2 tablespoons of oil in the casserole. Add the lamb cubes in a single layer without overcrowding the casserole, and cook until browned on each side; work in batches, if necessary.

3 Return the onion mixture to the casserole with all the lamb. Stir in the stock, wine, vinegar, tomatoes with their juices, and salt and pepper to taste. Bring to a boil, scraping any glazed bits from the bottom of the casserole. Reduce the heat and stir in the thyme, bay leaves, and paprika.

4 Transfer to a preheated oven, 325°F/160°C, and cook, covered, for 40–45 minutes until the lamb is tender. Stir in the chickpeas and return to the oven, uncovered, for 10 minutes, or until they are heated through and the juices are reduced.

5 Taste and adjust the seasoning. Garnish with thyme and serve.

roasted garlic-&-rosemary lamb with potatoes

ingredients

SERVES 6–8

15 garlic cloves, unpeeled, but separated into cloves

olive oil

1 leg of lamb, about 3 lb/1.3 kg

handful of fresh, tender rosemary sprigs

salt and pepper

24 new potatoes, scrubbed, but left whole

9 fl oz/250 ml/scant 1¼ cups full-bodied red wine, say one from Rioja or Navarre

method

1 Coat the garlic cloves with a little oil in your hands. Roast in a preheated oven, 400°F/200°C, for 20 minutes, or until very soft; cover with foil, if the cloves start to brown too much.

2 Let the garlic cool, then peel the cloves. Use a mortar and pestle to pound the garlic into a coarse paste with ½ teaspoon of oil. Make small incisions all over the lamb, then rub in the garlic paste. Let marinate for 2 hours.

3 Place the lamb in a roasting pan on a bed of rosemary sprigs, and season with salt and pepper. Rub the potatoes with oil and place round the lamb. Sprinkle with more rosemary and season to taste. Roast in a preheated oven, 450°F/230°C, for 10 minutes, then reduce the heat to 350°F/180°C for 15 minutes per 1 lb 2 oz/500 g plus an extra 15 minutes.

4 Let the lamb stand for 10 minutes before carving. If the potatoes are not tender, return them to the oven in a separate dish. Set aside the rosemary sprigs and skim off any fat in the pan. Pour in the wine and bring to a boil, scraping up any glazed bits from the bottom. Continue boiling until reduced to half. Taste and adjust the seasoning.

5 Slice the lamb and serve with the potatoes and juices spooned round.

chicken & duck paella with orange

ingredients

SERVES 4–6

1/2 tsp saffron threads

2 tbsp hot water

6 oz/175 g chicken breast, cut into bite-size chunks

4 large duck breasts, cut into bite-size chunks

2 tbsp olive oil

1 large onion, chopped

2 garlic cloves, crushed

1 tsp paprika

8 oz/225 g tomatoes, peeled and cut into wedges

1 orange bell pepper, seeded, broiled, peeled, and chopped coarsely

6 oz/175 g canned red kidney beans (drained weight)

13 oz/375 g/generous 1 1/2 cups paella rice

1 tbsp chopped parsley, plus extra sprigs to garnish

1 tbsp orange rind

2 tbsp orange juice

3 1/2 fl oz/100 ml/generous 1/3 cup white wine

2 pints/1.2 liters/5 cups simmering chicken stock

salt and pepper

orange wedges, to serve

method

1 Put the saffron threads and water in a small bowl and let infuse for a few minutes.

2 Season the chicken and duck to taste. Heat the oil in a large paella pan and cook the chicken and duck over medium-high heat, stirring, for 5 minutes, or until golden all over. Remove and set aside. Add the onion to the pan and stir over medium heat until softened. Add the garlic, paprika, and saffron and its soaking liquid and cook, stirring, for 1 minute. Add the tomato wedges, bell pepper, and beans and cook, stirring, for 2 minutes.

3 Add the rice and parsley and cook, stirring constantly, for 1 minute, to coat the rice. Add the orange rind and juice, wine, and most of the hot stock. Bring to a boil, then let simmer, uncovered, for 10 minutes. Do not stir during cooking, but shake the pan once or twice. Return the chicken and duck and any juices to the pan, give it a shake, and season. Cook for 10–15 minutes, or until the rice is almost cooked. Add a little more stock if necessary.

4 When all the liquid has been absorbed and you detect a faint toasty aroma coming from the rice, remove from the heat. Cover with foil and let stand for 5 minutes. Garnish with parsley sprigs and orange wedges.

outdoor paella

ingredients

SERVES 4–6

42 fl oz/1.25 liters/5¼ cups
    fish stock or water
12 large raw shrimp,
    in their shells
½ tsp saffron threads
2 tbsp hot water
3½ oz/100 g skinless, boneless
    chicken breast, cut into
    ½-inch/1-cm pieces
3½ oz/100 g pork tenderloin,
    cut into ½-inch/1-cm
    pieces
3 tbsp olive oil
3½ oz/100 g Spanish chorizo
    sausage, casing removed,
    cut into ½-inch/1-cm slices
1 large red onion, chopped
2 garlic cloves, crushed
½ tsp cayenne pepper
½ tsp paprika
1 red bell pepper and 1 green
    bell pepper, seeded
    and sliced
12 cherry tomatoes, halved
13 oz/375 g/generous
    1½ cups medium-grain
    paella rice
1 tbsp chopped fresh parsley
2 tsp chopped fresh tarragon
salt and pepper
1 lemon and 1 lime, cut into
    wedges, to serve

method

1 Put the stock in a pan and bring to a simmer. Add the shrimp and cook for 2 minutes, then transfer to a bowl and set aside. Let the stock simmer. Put the saffron threads and water in a bowl and let infuse.

2 Season the chicken and pork to taste. Heat the oil in a paella pan and cook the chicken, pork, and chorizo over medium heat, stirring, for 5 minutes, or until golden. Add the onion and cook, stirring, until softened. Add the garlic, cayenne pepper, paprika, and saffron and its soaking liquid and cook, stirring constantly, for 1 minute. Add the bell peppers and tomato halves and cook, stirring, for 2 minutes.

3 Add the rice and herbs and cook, stirring constantly, for 1 minute to coat. Pour in about 2 pints/1 liter/5 cups of the stock and bring to a boil, then simmer, uncovered, for 10 minutes. Do not stir during cooking, but shake the pan once or twice and when adding ingredients. Season to taste and cook for 10 minutes more, or until the rice grains are plump and almost cooked. Add a little more stock if necessary. Add the shrimp and cook for 2 minutes more.

4 When all the liquid has been absorbed and you detect a faint toasty aroma coming from the rice, remove from the heat immediately. Cover with foil and let stand for 5 minutes. Serve with the lemon and lime wedges.

paprika chicken on a bed of onions & ham

ingredients

SERVES 4

4 chicken breast fillets, skin on

5 fl oz/150 ml/$2/3$ cup freshly squeezed lemon juice

1–1$1/2$ tsp mild or hot Spanish paprika, to taste

salt and pepper

about 2 tbsp olive oil

2$1/2$ oz/70 g serrano ham or prosciutto, diced

4 large onions, sliced thinly

4 fl oz/125 ml/$1/2$ cup dry white wine

4 fl oz/125 ml/$1/2$ cup chicken stock

fresh thyme or chopped fresh parsley, to garnish

method

1 Pour the lemon juice over the chicken breasts in a nonmetallic bowl and let marinate in the refrigerator overnight.

2 Remove the chicken from the marinade and pat dry. Rub the skins with the paprika and season to taste. Heat 2 tablespoons of the oil in a large, lidded skillet over medium-high heat. Add the chicken breasts, skin-sides down, and cook for 5 minutes, or until the skins are golden; remove from the skillet.

3 Stir the ham into the fat remaining in the skillet, cover, and cook for about 2 minutes until it renders any fat. Add the onions and cook for about 5 minutes, stirring occasionally and adding a little extra oil if necessary, until the onions are soft, but not brown.

4 Add the wine and stock and bring to a boil, stirring. Return the chicken breasts to the skillet and season to taste. Reduce the heat, cover, and let simmer for 20 minutes, or until the chicken is cooked and the juices run clear. Remove and set aside in a warm oven.

5 Bring the sauce to a boil and let bubble until the juices reduce. Taste and adjust the seasoning. Divide the onion mixture between 4 warmed plates and arrange a chicken breast on top of each. Garnish with herbs to serve.

chicken with garlic

ingredients

SERVES 4–6

4 tbsp all-purpose flour

Spanish paprika, either hot or
    smoked sweet, to taste

salt and pepper

1 large chicken, about
    3³/₄ lb/1.75 kg, cut into
    8 pieces, rinsed,
    and patted dry

4–6 tbsp olive oil

24 large garlic cloves,
    peeled and halved

15 fl oz/450 ml/scant 2 cups
    chicken stock, preferably
    homemade

4 tbsp dry white wine,
    such as white Rioja

2 sprigs fresh parsley,
    1 bay leaf, and 1 sprig
    fresh thyme, tied together

fresh parsley and thyme
    leaves, to garnish

method

1 Sift the flour onto a large plate and season with paprika and salt and pepper to taste. Dredge the chicken pieces with the flour on both sides, shaking off the excess.

2 Heat 4 tablespoons of the oil in a large, deep skillet or flameproof casserole over medium heat. Add the garlic pieces and cook, stirring frequently, for about 2 minutes to flavor the oil. Remove with a slotted spoon and set aside to drain on paper towels.

3 Cook the chicken pieces, skin-side down, in a single layer, in batches if necessary, to avoid overcrowding the skillet, adding a little extra oil if necessary. Cook for 5 minutes until the skin is golden brown. Turn over and cook for 5 minutes longer.

4 Pour off any excess oil. Return the garlic and chicken pieces to the skillet and add the chicken stock, wine, and herbs. Bring to a boil, then reduce the heat, cover, and let simmer for 20–25 minutes, until the chicken is cooked through and the garlic very soft. Remove the chicken pieces and keep warm.

5 Bring the cooking liquid to a boil, with the garlic and herbs, and boil until reduced to about 10 fl oz/300 ml/ 1¹/₂ cups. Discard the herbs. Spoon the sauce and the garlic cloves over the chicken pieces. Garnish with the parsley and thyme, and serve.

cod with spinach

ingredients

SERVES 4
catalan spinach
2 oz/55g/$\frac{1}{2}$ cup raisins
2 oz/55g/$\frac{1}{3}$ cup pine nuts
4 tbsp extra-virgin olive oil
3 garlic cloves, crushed
1 lb 2oz/500 g/11$\frac{1}{4}$ cups
   baby spinach leaves,
   rinsed and shaken dry

4 cod fillets, each about
   6 oz/175 g
olive oil
salt and pepper
lemon wedges, to serve

method

1 Put the raisins for the Catalan spinach in a small bowl, cover with hot water, and set aside to soak for 15 minutes; drain well.

2 Meanwhile, put the pine nuts in a dry skillet over medium-high heat and dry-fry for 1–2 minutes, shaking frequently, until toasted and golden brown: watch closely because they burn quickly.

3 Heat the oil in a large, lidded skillet over medium-high heat. Add the garlic and cook for 2 minutes, or until golden, but not brown. Remove with a slotted spoon and discard.

4 Add the spinach to the oil with only the rinsing water clinging to its leaves. Cover and cook for 4–5 minutes until wilted. Uncover, stir in the drained raisins and pine nuts and continue cooking until all the liquid evaporates. Season to taste and keep warm.

5 To cook the cod, brush the fillets lightly with oil and sprinkle with salt and pepper. Place under a preheated hot broiler about 4 inches/10 cm from the heat and broil for 8–10 minutes until the flesh is opaque and flakes easily.

6 Divide the spinach between 4 plates and place the cod fillets on top. Serve with the lemon wedges.

seafood paella with lemon & herbs

ingredients

SERVES 4–6

$1/2$ tsp saffron threads

2 tbsp hot water

8 oz/225 g tomatoes, peeled
and cut into wedges

$5^1/2$ oz/150 g cod fillet, skinned
and rinsed under cold
running water

42 fl oz/1.25 liters/$5^1/2$ cups
simmering fish stock

12 large raw shrimp, shelled
and deveined

1 lb/450 g raw squid, cleaned
and cut into rings or
bite-size pieces
(or use the same quantity
of shelled scallops)

3 tbsp olive oil

1 large red onion, chopped

2 garlic cloves, crushed

1 small fresh red chile,
seeded and minced

13 oz/375 g/generous
$1^1/2$ cups medium-grain
paella rice

1 tbsp chopped fresh parsley

2 tsp chopped fresh dill

salt and pepper

1 lemon, cut into wedges,
to serve

method

1 Put the saffron threads and water in a small bowl and let infuse for a few minutes.

2 Add the cod to the pan of simmering stock and cook for 5 minutes, then transfer to a colander, rinse under cold running water and drain. Add the shrimp and squid to the stock and cook for 2 minutes. Cut the cod into chunks, then transfer with the other seafood to a bowl and set aside. Let the stock simmer.

3 Heat the oil in a paella pan and stir the onion over medium heat until softened. Add the garlic, chile, and saffron and its soaking liquid and cook, stirring, for 1 minute. Add the tomato wedges and cook, stirring, for 2 minutes. Add the rice and herbs and cook, stirring, for 1 minute. Add most of the stock and bring to a boil. Let simmer, uncovered, for 10 minutes. Do not stir during cooking, but shake the pan once or twice and when adding ingredients. Season and cook for 10 minutes, until the rice is almost cooked. Add more stock if necessary. Add the seafood and cook for 2 minutes.

4 When all the liquid has been absorbed and you detect a faint toasty aroma coming from the rice, remove from the heat immediately. Cover with foil and let stand for 5 minutes. Serve with the lemon wedges.

roast monkfish with romesco sauce

ingredients

SERVES 4–6

2 lb/900 g monkfish in 1 piece

2–3 slices serrano ham or
    prosciutto

olive oil

salt and pepper

1 x recipe Romesco Sauce,
    to serve (see page 198)

method

1 Remove the thin membrane covering the monkfish, then rinse the tail and pat it dry. Wrap the ham round the monkfish and rub lightly with oil. Season with salt and pepper. Put on a baking sheet.

2 Roast the monkfish in a preheated oven, 400°F/200°C, for 20 minutes until the flesh is opaque and flakes easily: test by lifting off the ham along the central bone and cut a small amount of the flesh away from the bone to see if it flakes.

3 Cut through the ham to remove the central bone and produce 2 thick fillets. Cut each fillet into 2 or 3 pieces and arrange on a plate with a spoonful of Romesco Sauce. Serve at once.

spanish swordfish stew

ingredients

SERVES 4

4 tbsp olive oil

3 shallots, chopped

2 garlic cloves, chopped

8 oz/225 g canned chopped
    tomatoes

1 tbsp tomato paste

1 lb 7 oz/650 g potatoes, sliced

9 fl oz/250 ml/generous 1 cup
    vegetable stock

2 tbsp lemon juice

1 red bell pepper, seeded and
    chopped

1 orange bell pepper, seeded
    and chopped

20 black olives, pitted
    and halved

2 lb 4 oz/1 kg swordfish
    steak, skinned and cut
    into bite-size pieces

salt and pepper

crusty bread, to serve

to garnish

fresh flat-leaf parsley sprigs

lemon slices

method

1 Heat the oil in a pan over low heat, add the shallots, and cook, stirring frequently, for 4 minutes, or until softened. Add the garlic, tomatoes, and tomato paste, cover, and let simmer gently for 20 minutes.

2 Meanwhile, put the potatoes in an ovenproof casserole with the stock and lemon juice. Bring to a boil, then reduce the heat and add the bell peppers. Cover and cook for 15 minutes.

3 Add the olives, swordfish, and the tomato mixture to the potatoes. Season to taste with salt and pepper. Stir well, then cover and let simmer for 7–10 minutes, or until the swordfish is cooked to your taste.

4 Remove from the heat and garnish with parsley sprigs and lemon slices. Serve with crusty bread.

catalan fish stew

ingredients

SERVES 4–6

large pinch of saffron threads

6 tbsp olive oil

1 large onion, chopped

2 garlic cloves, chopped finely

1^1/$_2$ tbsp chopped fresh
    thyme leaves

2 bay leaves

2 red bell peppers, cored,
    seeded, and chopped
    coarsely

1 lb 12 oz/800 g canned
    chopped tomatoes

1 tsp sweet smoked paprika

9 fl oz/250 ml/scant 1^1/$_4$ cups
    fish stock

5 oz/140 g/1 cup blanched
    almonds, toasted and
    ground finely

salt and pepper

12–16 live mussels with
    tightly closed shells

12–16 live clams with tightly
    closed shells

1 lb 5 oz/600 g thick, boned
    hake or cod fillets, skinned
    and cut into 2-inch/5-cm
    chunks

12–16 uncooked shrimp,
    heads and tails removed
    and deveined

crusty bread, to serve

method

1 Infuse the saffron threads in 4 tablespoons of boiling water in a heatproof bowl.

2 Heat the oil in a heavy-bottom flameproof casserole over medium-high heat. Reduce the heat to low, add the onion, and cook for 10 minutes, or until golden, but not brown. Stir in the garlic, thyme, bay leaves, and red bell peppers and continue cooking for an additional 5 minutes, or until the bell peppers are soft and the onions have softened further. Add the tomatoes and paprika and continue to simmer for 5 minutes, stirring frequently.

3 Stir in the fish stock, reserved saffron water, and ground almonds, and bring to a boil, stirring frequently. Reduce the heat and let simmer for 5–10 minutes until the sauce reduces and thickens. Season to taste.

4 Meanwhile, prepare the mussels and clams, discarding any with cracked shells and any open ones that do not close when tapped. Cut off and discard any beards from the mussels, then scrub any dirty shells.

5 Gently stir in the hake and add the shrimp, mussels, and clams. Reduce the heat to very low, cover the casserole, and let simmer for about 5 minutes until the hake is cooked through, the shrimp turn pink and the mussels and clams open; discard any that remain closed. Serve at once with the bread.

flounder for two

ingredients

SERVES 2

5 fl oz/150 ml/²/₃ cup olive oil

13 oz/375 g waxy potatoes,
    peeled and sliced thinly

1 fennel bulb, trimmed and
    sliced thinly

2 large tomatoes, broiled and
    peeled, seeded,
    and chopped

2 shallots, sliced

salt and pepper

1 or 2 whole flounder, about
    3 lb/1.3 kg, cleaned

4 tbsp dry white wine

2 tbsp finely chopped
    fresh parsley

lemon wedges, to serve

method

1 Spread 4 tablespoons of the oil over the bottom in a shallow roasting pan large enough to hold the flounder. Arrange the potatoes in a single layer, then top with the fennel, tomatoes, and shallots. Season with salt and pepper. Drizzle with an additional 4 tablespoons of the oil. Roast the vegetables in a preheated oven, 400°F/200°C, for 30 minutes.

2 Season the fish with salt and pepper and put on top of the vegetables. Sprinkle with the wine and the remaining 2 tablespoons of oil.

3 Return the roasting pan to the oven and roast the fish, uncovered, for 20 minutes, or until the flesh flakes easily. To serve, skin the fish and remove the fillets. Sprinkle the parsley over the vegetables. Arrange 2–4 fillets on each plate, with the vegetables spooned alongside, and the lemon wedges.

hake in white wine

ingredients

SERVES 4

about 2 tbsp all-purpose flour

4 hake fillets, about
    5 oz/150 g each

4 tbsp extra-virgin olive oil

4 fl oz/125ml/$\frac{1}{2}$ cup dry
    white wine, such as a
    white Rioja

2 large garlic cloves,
    chopped very finely

6 scallions, sliced finely

2 tbsp fresh parsley,
    chopped very finely

salt and pepper

method

1 Season the flour generously with salt and pepper on a flat plate. Dredge the skin side of the hake fillets in the seasoned flour, then shake off the excess; set aside.

2 Heat a shallow, flameproof casserole over high heat until you can feel the heat rising. Add the oil and heat for about 30 seconds, until a cube of day-old bread sizzles. Add the hake fillets, skin-side down, and cook for 3 minutes until the skin is golden brown.

3 Turn the fish over and season with salt and pepper to taste. Pour in the wine and add the garlic, scallions, and parsley. Transfer the casserole, uncovered, to a preheated oven, 450°F/230°C, and bake for 5 minutes, or until the flesh flakes easily. Serve straight from the casserole.

roasted tuna with orange & anchovies

ingredients

SERVES 4–6

7 fl oz/200 ml/scant 1 cup
  freshly squeezed
  orange juice

3 tbsp extra-virgin olive oil

2 oz/55 g anchovy fillets in oil,
  chopped coarsely, with the
  oil set aside

small pinch dried red pepper
  flakes, or to taste

pepper

1 tuna fillet, about 20 oz/600 g

method

1 Combine the orange juice, 2 tablespoons of the olive oil, the anchovies and their oil, the red pepper flakes, and pepper to taste in a large nonmetallic bowl. Add the tuna and spoon over the marinade. Cover and let chill in the refrigerator for at least 2 hours, turning the tuna occasionally. Remove 20 minutes before cooking to bring the fish to room temperature, then remove from the marinade and wipe dry.

2 Heat the remaining tablespoon of olive oil in a large skillet over high heat. Add the tuna and sear for 1 minute on each side until lightly browned and crisp. Place the tuna in a small roasting pan and cover the pan tightly with foil.

3 Roast in a preheated oven, 425°F/220°C, for 8 minutes for medium-rare and 10 minutes for medium-well done. Remove from the oven and set aside to rest for at least 2 minutes before carving. Meanwhile, put the marinade in a small pan over high heat and bring to a rolling boil. Boil for at least 2 minutes.

4 Transfer the tuna to a serving platter and carve into thick slices, which will probably break into chunks as you cut them. Serve the sauce separately for spooning over.

basque tuna stew

ingredients

SERVES 4

5 tbsp olive oil

1 large onion, chopped

2 garlic cloves, chopped

7 oz/200 g canned chopped
   tomatoes

1 lb 9 oz/700 g potatoes, cut
   into 2-inch/5-cm chunks

3 green bell peppers, seeded
   and coarsely chopped

10 fl oz/300 ml/1¼ cups
   cold water

2 lb/900 g fresh tuna,
   cut into chunks

4 slices crusty white bread

salt and pepper

method

1 Heat 2 tablespoons of the oil in a pan over medium heat, add the onion, and cook, stirring frequently, for 8–10 minutes until softened and browned. Add the garlic and cook, stirring, for an additional minute. Add the tomatoes, cover, and let simmer for 30 minutes, or until thickened.

2 Meanwhile, in a separate pan, mix together the potatoes and bell peppers. Add the water (which should just cover the vegetables) and bring to a boil, then reduce the heat and let simmer for 15 minutes, or until the potatoes are almost tender.

3 Add the tuna and the tomato mixture to the potatoes and bell peppers and season to taste with salt and pepper. Cover and simmer for 6–8 minutes until the tuna is tender.

4 Meanwhile, heat the remaining oil in a large skillet over medium heat, add the bread slices, and cook on both sides until golden. Remove with a slotted spoon and drain on paper towels. Serve with the stew.

salmon steaks with green sauce

ingredients

SERVES 4

green sauce

2¹/₂ oz/70 g/generous 4 tbsp sprigs fresh flat-leaf parsley

8 large fresh basil leaves

2 sprigs fresh oregano, or ¹/₂ tsp dried

3–4 anchovy fillets in oil, drained and chopped

2 tsp capers in brine, rinsed

1 shallot, chopped

1 large garlic clove

2–3 tsp lemon juice, to taste

4 fl oz/125ml/¹/₂ cup extra-virgin olive oil

4 skinned salmon fillets, each about 5 oz/150 g

2 tbsp olive oil

salt and pepper

method

1 To make the green sauce, put the parsley, basil, oregano, anchovies, capers, shallot, garlic, and lemon juice in a food processor or blender and process until chopped. With the motor running, slowly add the oil through the feed tube. Taste and adjust the seasoning, if necessary, remembering that the anchovies and capers can be salty. Pour into a serving bowl, cover with plastic wrap and let chill until required.

2 When ready to serve, brush the salmon fillets on both sides with the olive oil and season with salt and pepper to taste. Heat a large skillet until you can feel the heat rising from the surface. Add the salmon steaks and cook for 3 minutes. Flip the steaks over and continue cooking for 2–3 minutes until they feel springy and the flesh flakes easily.

3 Serve the hot salmon steaks with a little of the chilled sauce spooned over.

paprika shrimp

ingredients

SERVES 4–6

16–24 large, uncooked
    jumbo shrimp
6 tbsp extra-virgin olive oil
1 large garlic clove, crushed
$\frac{1}{2}$ tsp mild paprika, or to taste
salt
lemon wedges, to serve

method

1 Remove the shell from the center of the shrimp, leaving the heads and tails intact. Devein the shrimp.

2 Mix together the oil, garlic, paprika, and salt in a shallow dish large enough to hold the shrimp in a single layer. Stir together, then add the shrimp and turn so they are coated. Cover with plastic wrap and let marinate in the fridge for at least 1 hour.

3 When ready to cook, heat a large, ridged cast-iron grill pan over medium-high heat until you can feel the heat rising. Add as many shrimp as will fit without overcrowding the grill pan. Cook about 1 minute until the shrimp curl and the shells turn pink. Turn over and continue cooking for an additional minute, or until cooked through. Drain well on paper towels and keep hot while you continue cooking the remainder.

4 Serve at once with lemon wedges for squeezing over the shrimp.

spaghetti with shrimp

ingredients

SERVES 4

1 lb/450 g dried spaghetti

4 fl oz/125 ml/$\frac{1}{2}$ cup olive oil

6 garlic cloves, sliced thinly

1 lb/450 g medium uncooked
    shrimp, shelled and
    deveined

2 tbsp flat-leaf parsley,
    chopped finely, plus 2 tbsp
    extra for garnishing

4 fl oz/125 ml/$\frac{1}{2}$ cup dry
    white wine

4 tbsp freshly squeezed
    lemon juice

salt and pepper

method

1 Bring a large pan of salted water to a boil over high heat. Add the spaghetti, return the water to a boil, and continue boiling for 10 minutes (check the package instructions), or until tender.

2 Meanwhile, heat the oil in another large pan over medium heat. Add the garlic and cook until just golden brown. Add the shrimp and 2 tablespoons of chopped parsley and stir. Add the wine and let simmer for 2 minutes. Stir in the lemon juice and simmer until the shrimp turn pink and curl.

3 Drain the spaghetti. Tip into the pan with the shrimp and toss. Add salt and pepper to taste.

4 Transfer to a large serving platter and sprinkle with the extra parsley. Serve at once.

black rice

ingredients

SERVES 4–6

14 oz/400 g/scant 2 cups
    Spanish short-grain rice

6 tbsp olive oil

1 large onion, sliced finely

2 large garlic cloves, crushed

2 tomatoes, broiled, peeled,
    seeded, and chopped finely

1 prepared squid body, cut
    into 1/4-inch/5-mm rings
    (tentacles set aside,
    if available)

1 3/4 pints/1 liter/4 cups
    fish stock

ink sac from squid, or a sachet
    of squid ink

salt and pepper

12 large uncooked shrimp,
    shelled and deveined

squid tentacles, if available

2 red bell peppers, broiled,
    peeled, seeded and sliced

garlic mayonnaise, to serve
    (see page 200)

method

1 Put the rice in a strainer and rinse until the water runs clear; set aside.

2 Heat the oil in a large, shallow casserole or skillet over medium-high heat. Add the onion and cook for 3 minutes, then add the garlic cloves and cook for an additional 2 minutes until the onion is soft, but not brown. Add the tomatoes and let simmer until they are very soft. Add the squid rings and cook quickly until they turn opaque.

3 Add the rice and stir until it is coated in oil. Pour in the stock, squid ink, and salt and pepper to taste and bring to a boil. Reduce the heat and let simmer for 15 minutes, uncovered and without stirring, but shaking the skillet frequently, until most of the stock is absorbed and small holes appear on the surface.

4 Lightly stir in the shrimp, squid tentacles, if using, and bell peppers. Cover the skillet and continue simmering for about 5 minutes until the shrimp turn pink and the tentacles turn opaque and curl.

5 Taste and adjust the seasoning. Serve with garlic mayonnaise on the side of each plate.

on the side

A most amazing range of vegetables is grown in Spain and they are only eaten when in season. Potatoes, of course, have been a favorite ever since they were introduced by Christopher Columbus more than five hundred years ago. If you love the intense heat of chiles, try Feisty Potatoes—you won't have to ask how they got their name! As is very often the case, every cook in Spain claims that his or her recipe for this dish is the authentic one.

Although you won't find many vegetarian dishes in the Spanish cook's repertoire, it is still possible to create a really interesting and appetizing vegetable-based meal. Eggplants, introduced by the Moors, are typically marinated in olive oil flavored with garlic, fresh herbs, and lemon, then roasted in the oven. They soak up the oil and are delicious served just warm. Green beans are cooked until just tender and are extra good if they are then tossed in lemony butter with some flaked almonds, which gives them an added texture, or served with some roasted pine nuts scattered over. Mushrooms stuffed with bread crumbs mixed with a rich garlic butter with fresh thyme are fabulous, and Spinach with Chickpeas provide another source of protein. Add some of those Feisty Potatoes, and there won't be too many complaints!

pan-fried potatoes with piquant paprika

ingredients

SERVES 6

3 tsp paprika

1 tsp ground cumin

$1/4$–$1/2$ tsp cayenne pepper

$1/2$ tsp salt

1 lb/450 g small old potatoes, peeled

corn oil, for pan-frying

sprigs of fresh flat-leaf parsley, to garnish

garlic mayonnaise, to serve (optional, see page 200)

method

1 Put the paprika, cumin, cayenne pepper, and salt in a small bowl and mix well together. Set aside.

2 Cut each potato into 8 thick wedges. Pour corn oil into a large, heavy-bottom skillet to a depth of about 1 inch/2.5 cm. Heat the oil, then add the potato wedges, preferably in a single layer, and cook gently for 10 minutes, or until golden brown all over, turning from time to time. Remove from the skillet with a slotted spoon and let drain on paper towels.

3 Transfer the potato wedges to a large bowl and, while they are still hot, sprinkle with the paprika mixture, then gently toss them together to coat.

4 Turn the potatoes into a large, warmed serving dish and serve hot, garnished with parsley sprigs. Accompany with a bowl of garlic mayonnaise, if wished.

"wrinkled" potatoes with mojo sauce

ingredients

SERVES 4–6

2$\frac{1}{2}$ oz/70 g/generous $\frac{1}{3}$ cup sea salt

24 small, new red-skinned potatoes, unpeeled and kept whole

mojo sauce

1$\frac{1}{2}$ oz/40 g day-old bread, crusts removed and torn into small pieces

2 large garlic cloves

$\frac{1}{2}$ tsp salt

1$\frac{1}{2}$ tbsp hot Spanish paprika

1 tbsp ground cumin

approx 2 tbsp red wine vinegar

approx 5 tbsp extra-virgin olive oil

2 pimientos del piquillo, preserved, drained

method

1 Pour about 1 inch/2.5 cm water into a pan and stir in the sea salt. Add the potatoes and stir again: they do not have to be covered with water. Fit a clean dish towel over the potatoes, then bring the water to a boil. Reduce the heat and let simmer for 20 minutes, or until the potatoes are tender, but still holding together.

2 Remove the dish towel and set aside to cool. Drain the potatoes and return them to the pan. Wring the saltwater from the dish towel into the pan. Put the pan over low heat and shake until the potatoes are dry and coated with a thin white film. Remove from the heat.

3 To make the mojo sauce, put the bread in a bowl and add just enough water to cover. Set aside for 5 minutes to soften, then squeeze out all the water. Use a mortar and pestle to mash the garlic and salt into a paste. Stir in the paprika and cumin. Transfer to a food processor. Add 2 tablespoons of vinegar and blend, then add the bread and 2 tablespoons of oil and blend again.

4 With the motor running, add the pepper pieces a few at a time until they are puréed and a sauce forms. Add more oil, if necessary, until the sauce is smooth and thick. Serve the potatoes hot or warm with the mojo sauce.

pan-fried potatoes

ingredients

SERVES 6

2 lb 4 oz/1 kg potatoes,
    unpeeled

olive oil

sea salt

method

1 Scrub the potatoes, pat them dry, and cut into chunky pieces.

2 Put $1/2$ inch/1 cm olive oil and 1 potato piece in 1 or 2 large, heavy-bottom skillets over medium-high heat and heat until the potato starts to sizzle. Add the remaining potatoes, without crowding the skillets, and cook for about 15 minutes until golden brown all over and tender. Work in batches, if necessary, keeping the cooked potatoes warm while you cook the remainder.

3 Use a slotted spoon to transfer the potatoes to a plate covered with crumpled paper towels. Blot off any excess oil and sprinkle with sea salt. Serve at once.

feisty potatoes

ingredients

SERVES 6

chili oil

¼ pint/150 ml/⅔ cup
    olive oil

2 small, hot red chiles, slit

1 tsp hot Spanish paprika

1 x quantity pan-fried
    potatoes (see page 164)

1 x quantity garlic
    mayonnaise (see page
    200)

method

1 To make the chili oil, heat the oil and chiles over high heat until the chiles start to sizzle. Remove from the heat and stir in the paprika. Set aside and let cool, then transfer to a pourer with a spout; do not strain.

2 Serve the pan-fried potatoes warm or at room temperature, drizzled with the chili oil and accompanied with the garlic mayonnaise.

mixed vegetable stew

ingredients

SERVES 4–6

about 4 fl oz/125 ml/$1/2$ cup
   olive oil

2 large onions, sliced thinly

4 large garlic cloves, crushed

10 oz/300 g eggplant, cut into
   $1/2$-inch/1-cm cubes

10 oz/300 g yellow or green
   zucchini, cut into
   $1/2$-inch/1-cm cubes

1 large red bell pepper, cored,
   seeded, and chopped

1 large yellow bell pepper,
   cored, seeded,
   and chopped

1 large green bell pepper,
   cored, seeded,
   and chopped

2 sprigs fresh thyme

1 bay leaf

1 small sprig young rosemary

$3 1/2$ fl oz/100 ml/generous
   $1/3$ cup vegetable stock

salt and pepper

1 lb/450 g large, juicy tomatoes,
   peeled, seeded,
   and chopped

method

1 Heat about 2 tablespoons of the oil in a large, flameproof casserole over medium heat. Add the onions and cook, stirring occasionally, about 5 minutes until they start to soften, but not brown. Add the garlic and stir round. Reduce the heat to very low.

2 Meanwhile, heat a skillet over high heat until you can feel the heat rising. Add 1 tablespoon of the oil and the eggplant cubes to make a single layer. Cook, stirring, until they are slightly brown on all sides. Add to the casserole with the onions.

3 Add another tablespoon of oil to the skillet. Add the zucchini and cook, stirring, until lightly browned all over. Add the zucchini to the casserole. Cook the bell peppers the same way, then add to the casserole.

4 Stir the thyme, bay leaf, rosemary, stock, and salt and pepper to taste into the casserole and bring to a boil. Reduce the heat to very low again, cover, and let simmer, stirring occasionally, for about 20 minutes until the vegetables are very tender and blended.

5 Remove the casserole from the heat and stir in the tomatoes. Cover and set aside for 10 minutes for the tomatoes to soften. The stew is now ready to serve, but it is even better if it is left to cool completely and then served chilled the next day.

spinach with chickpeas

ingredients

SERVES 4–6

2 tbsp olive oil

1 large garlic clove, cut in half

1 medium onion,
    chopped finely

$1/2$ tsp cumin

pinch cayenne pepper

pinch turmeric

1 lb 12 oz/800 g canned
    chickpeas, drained
    and rinsed

18 oz/500 g/$11^{1}/_{4}$ cups
    baby spinach leaves,
    rinsed and shaken dry

2 pimientos del piquillo,
    drained and sliced

salt and pepper

method

1 Heat the oil in a large, lidded skillet over medium-high heat. Add the garlic and cook for 2 minutes, or until golden, but not brown. Remove with a slotted spoon and discard.

2 Add the onion and cumin, cayenne and turmeric and cook, stirring, for about 5 minutes until soft. Add the chickpeas and stir round until they are lightly colored with the turmeric and cayenne.

3 Stir in the spinach with just the water clinging to its leaves. Cover and cook for 4–5 minutes until wilted. Uncover, stir in the pimientos del piquillo and continue cooking, stirring gently, until all the liquid evaporates. Season to taste and serve.

green beans with almonds

ingredients

SERVES 4–6

1 lb 2 oz/500 g green beans

2 oz/55 g butter

1 oz/25 g slivered almonds

2 tsp lemon juice

salt

method

1 Bring a pan of lightly salted water to a boil. Add the beans and let simmer for 8–10 minutes, or until just tender but still retaining a slight "bite."

2 Meanwhile, melt the butter in a heavy-bottom skillet. Add the almonds and cook over low heat, stirring frequently, for 3–5 minutes, or until golden. Stir in the lemon juice and season to taste with salt.

3 Drain the beans and add to the skillet. Stir well to mix, then transfer to individual serving dishes and serve warm.

green beans with pine nuts

ingredients

SERVES 8

2 tbsp Spanish olive oil

1³/₄ oz/50 g/scant ¹/₃ cup
   pine nuts

¹/₂–1 tsp paprika

1 lb/450 g green beans

1 small onion, finely chopped

1 garlic clove, finely chopped

salt and pepper

juice of ¹/₂ lemon

method

1 Heat the oil in a large, heavy-bottom skillet, add the pine nuts and cook for about 1 minute, stirring all the time and shaking the skillet, until light golden brown. Using a slotted spoon, remove the pine nuts from the skillet, drain well on paper towels, then transfer to a bowl. Set aside the oil in the skillet for later. Add the paprika, according to taste, to the pine nuts, stir together until coated, and then set aside.

2 Trim the green beans and remove any strings if necessary. Put the beans in a pan, pour over boiling water, return to a boil, and cook for 5 minutes, or until tender but still firm. Drain well in a strainer.

3 Reheat the oil in the skillet, add the onion and cook for 5–10 minutes, or until softened and starting to brown. Add the garlic and cook for an additional 30 seconds.

4 Add the beans to the skillet and cook for 2–3 minutes, tossing together with the onion until heated through. Season the beans to taste with salt and pepper.

5 Turn the contents of the skillet into a warmed serving dish, sprinkle over the lemon juice, and toss together. Sprinkle over the golden pine nuts and serve hot.

mixed beans

ingredients

SERVES 4–6

6 oz/175 g shelled fresh or
   frozen fava beans
4 oz/115 g fresh or frozen
   green beans
4 oz/115 g snow peas
1 shallot, finely chopped
6 fresh mint sprigs
4 tbsp olive oil
1 tbsp sherry vinegar
1 garlic clove, finely chopped
salt and pepper

method

1 Bring a large pan of lightly salted water to a boil. Add the fava beans and reduce the heat, then cover and simmer for 7 minutes. Remove the beans with a slotted spoon, then plunge into cold water and drain. Remove and discard the outer skins.

2 Meanwhile, return the pan of salted water to a boil. Add the green beans and return to a boil again. Drain and refresh under cold running water. Drain well.

3 Mix the fava beans, green beans, snow peas, and shallot together in a bowl. Strip the leaves from the mint sprigs, then reserve half and add the remainder to the bean mixture. Finely chop the reserved mint.

4 Whisk the olive oil, vinegar, garlic, and chopped mint together in a separate bowl and season to taste with salt and pepper. Pour the dressing over the bean mixture and toss lightly to coat. Cover with plastic wrap and let chill until required.

fava beans with serrano ham

ingredients

SERVES 6–8

2 oz/55 g serrano or prosciutto, pancetta, or rindless smoked lean bacon

4 oz/115 g chorizo sausage, outer casing removed

4 tbsp Spanish olive oil

1 onion, finely chopped

2 garlic cloves, finely chopped

splash of dry white wine

1 lb/450 g frozen fava beans, thawed, or about 3 lb/1.3 kg fresh fava beans in their pods, shelled to give 1 lb/450 g

1 tbsp chopped fresh mint or dill, plus extra to garnish

pinch of sugar

salt and pepper

method

1 Using a sharp knife, cut the ham, pancetta, or bacon into small strips. Cut the chorizo into 3/4-inch/2-cm cubes. Heat the olive oil in a large, heavy-bottom skillet or ovenproof dish that has a lid. Add the onion and cook for 5 minutes, or until softened and starting to brown. If you are using pancetta or bacon, add it with the onion. Add the garlic and cook for 30 seconds.

2 Pour the wine into the skillet, increase the heat, and let it bubble to evaporate the alcohol, then lower the heat. Add the fava beans, ham, if using, and the chorizo and cook for 1–2 minutes, stirring all the time to coat in the oil.

3 Cover the skillet and let the beans simmer very gently in the oil, stirring from time to time, for 10–15 minutes, or until the beans are tender, adding a little water if the beans become too dry. Stir in the mint or dill and sugar. Season the dish with salt, if necessary, and pepper.

4 Transfer the fava beans to a large, warmed serving dish, several smaller ones, or individual plates and serve piping hot, garnished with chopped mint or dill.

marinated eggplants

ingredients

SERVES 4

2 eggplants, halved lengthwise

4 tbsp olive oil

2 garlic cloves, finely chopped

2 tbsp chopped fresh parsley

1 tbsp chopped fresh thyme

2 tbsp lemon juice

salt and pepper

method

1 Make 2–3 slashes in the flesh of the eggplant halves and place, cut-side down, in an ovenproof dish. Season to taste with salt and pepper, then pour over the olive oil and sprinkle with the garlic, parsley, and thyme. Cover and let marinate at room temperature for 2–3 hours.

2 Uncover the dish and roast the eggplants in a preheated oven, 350°F/180°C, for 45 minutes. Remove the dish from the oven and turn the eggplants over. Baste with the cooking juices and sprinkle with the lemon juice. Return to the oven and cook for 15 minutes.

3 Transfer the eggplants to serving plates. Spoon over the cooking juices and serve hot or warm.

artichoke hearts & peas

ingredients

SERVES 4–6

4 tbsp extra-virgin olive oil

2 onions, sliced finely

1 large garlic clove, crushed

10 oz/280 g artichoke hearts
    preserved in oil, drained
    and halved

7 oz/200 g/1¾ cups frozen or
    fresh shelled peas

2 red bell peppers, broiled,
    seeded, and sliced

2 thin slices serrano ham,
    chopped (optional),
    or prosciutto

6 tbsp finely chopped
    fresh parsley

juice ½ lemon

salt and pepper

method

1 Heat the oil in a flameproof casserole over medium-high heat. Add the onions and cook, stirring, for 3 minutes, then add the garlic and cook for 2 minutes until the onions are soft, but not brown.

2 Add the halved artichoke hearts and fresh peas, if using, along with just enough water to cover. Bring to a boil, then reduce the heat and let simmer for 5 minutes, uncovered, or until the peas are cooked through and all the water has evaporated.

3 Stir in the bell peppers, ham, and frozen peas, if using. Continue simmering just long enough to warm through. Stir in the parsley and lemon juice to taste. Add salt and pepper, remembering that the ham is salty. Serve at once, or let cool to room temperature.

stuffed mushrooms

ingredients

SERVES 6

6 oz/175 g butter

4 garlic cloves, finely chopped

6 large open mushrooms,
   stems removed

2 oz/55 g/1 cup fresh white
   bread crumbs

1 tbsp chopped fresh thyme

1 egg, lightly beaten

salt and pepper

method

1 Cream the butter in a bowl until softened, then beat in the garlic. Divide two-thirds of the garlic butter between the mushroom caps and arrange them, cup-side up, on a baking sheet.

2 Melt the remaining garlic butter in a heavy-bottom or nonstick skillet. Add the bread crumbs and cook over low heat, stirring frequently, until golden. Remove from the heat and tip into a bowl. Stir in the thyme and season to taste with salt and pepper. Stir in the beaten egg until thoroughly combined.

3 Divide the bread-crumb mixture between the mushroom caps and bake in a preheated oven, 350°F/180°C, for 15 minutes, or until the stuffing is golden brown and the mushrooms are tender. Serve hot or warm.

stuffed tomatoes with rice

ingredients

SERVES 4

5 oz/140 g/³/₄ cup
  long-grain rice

5 oz/140 g/generous ¹/₄ cup
  black olives, pitted and
  chopped

3 tbsp olive oil

4 beef or other large
  tomatoes, halved

4 tbsp chopped fresh parsley

salt and pepper

method

1 Bring a large pan of lightly salted water to a boil. Add the rice, return to a boil, and stir once. Reduce the heat and cook for 10–15 minutes, or until only just tender. Drain well, rinse under cold running water, and drain again. Line a large, shallow dish with paper towels, then spread out the rice on top for about 1 hour to dry.

2 Mix the rice, olives, and olive oil together in a bowl and season well with pepper. You will probably not require any additional salt. Cover with plastic wrap and let stand at room temperature for 8 hours or overnight.

3 Cut a slice off the tops of the tomatoes and, using a teaspoon, carefully scoop out and discard the seeds without piercing the shells. Scoop out the flesh, finely chop, and add to the rice and olive mixture. Season the insides of the shells to taste with salt, then turn them upside down on paper towels and let drain for 1 hour.

4 Pat the insides of the tomato shells dry with paper towels, then divide the rice and olive mixture between them. Sprinkle with the parsley and serve.

sweet onion salad

ingredients

SERVES 4–6

4 Spanish onions

2 tbsp chopped fresh parsley

4oz/115 g/^{2}/$_3$ cup black
    olives, pitted

1 tbsp sherry vinegar

2 tbsp red wine vinegar

4 fl oz/125 ml/^{1}/$_2$ cup olive oil

about 1 tbsp water

salt and pepper

method

1 Bring a large pan of lightly salted water to a boil. Add the onions and simmer for 20 minutes, or until tender. Drain and let stand until cool enough to handle.

2 Thickly slice the onions and place in a shallow dish. Sprinkle over the parsley and olives and season to taste with pepper.

3 Whisk the vinegars and olive oil together in a bowl, then whisk in enough of the water to make a creamy vinaigrette. Pour the dressing over the onions and serve at room temperature.

orange & fennel salad

ingredients

SERVES 4

4 large, juicy oranges

1 large fennel bulb,
    sliced very thinly

1 mild white onion, sliced finely

2 tbsp extra-virgin olive oil

12 plump black olives, pitted
    and sliced thinly

1 fresh red chile, seeded and
    sliced very thinly (optional)

finely chopped fresh parsley

French bread, to serve

method

1 Finely grate the rind from the oranges into a bowl; set aside. Using a small serrated knife, remove all the white pith from the oranges, working over a bowl to catch the juices. Cut the oranges horizontally into thin slices.

2 Toss the orange slices with the fennel and onion slices. Whisk the oil into the reserved orange juice, then spoon over the oranges. Sprinkle the olive slices over the top, add the chile, if using, then sprinkle with the orange rind and parsley.

3 Serve with slices of French bread.

saffron rice with green vegetables

ingredients

SERVES 4–6

large pinch saffron threads
2 pints/1.2 liters/5 cups
    vegetable stock, hot
2 tbsp extra-virgin olive oil
1 large onion, chopped finely
1 large garlic clove, crushed
14 oz/400 g/scant 2 cups
    short-grain Spanish rice
$3^1/_2$ oz/100 g thin green
    beans, chopped
salt and pepper
$3^1/_2$ oz/100 g/scant 1 cup
    frozen peas
flat-leaf parsley, to garnish

method

1 Put the saffron threads in a heatproof bowl and add the hot vegetable stock; set aside to infuse.

2 Meanwhile, heat the oil in a shallow, heavy-bottom flameproof casserole over medium-high heat. Add the onion and cook for about 3 minutes, then add the garlic and cook for an additional 2 minutes, or until the onion is soft, but not brown.

3 Rinse the rice until the water runs clear. Drain, then add with the beans and stir until they are coated with oil. Pour in the stock with salt and pepper to taste and bring to a boil. Reduce the heat and let simmer for 12 minutes, uncovered, and without stirring.

4 Gently stir in the peas and continue simmering for 8 minutes until the liquid has been absorbed and the beans and peas are tender. Taste and adjust the seasoning. Garnish with the parsley and serve.

sherry rice

ingredients

SERVES 4–6

2 tbsp olive oil

1 large onion, chopped finely

1 large garlic clove, crushed

14 oz/400 g/scant 2 cups
    Spanish short-grain rice

8 fl oz/225 ml/1 cup
    amontillado sherry

1³/₄ pints/1 liter/4 cups fresh
    chicken stock, hot

pinch of cayenne pepper

salt and pepper

method

1 Heat the oil in a shallow, heavy-bottom flameproof casserole. Add the onion and cook for 3 minutes, then add the garlic and cook for an additional 2 minutes, or until the onion is soft, but not brown.

2 Rinse the rice until the water runs clear. Drain, then add to the casserole and stir until it is coated in the oil. Add all but 2 tablespoons of the sherry and let it bubble. Pour in the stock with the cayenne and salt and pepper to taste and bring to a boil. Reduce the heat and let simmer for 20 minutes, uncovered and without stirring, until most of the stock is absorbed and small holes appear on the surface.

3 Turn off the heat under the rice, sprinkle with the remaining sherry, cover, and let stand for 10 minutes until all the liquid is absorbed.

tomato & bell pepper sauce

ingredients

**MAKES ABOUT 1 1/4 PINTS/
675 ML/3 CUPS**

4 tbsp olive oil

10 large garlic cloves

5 oz/140 g shallots, chopped

4 large red bell peppers, cored,
    seeded, and chopped

2 lb 4 oz/1 kg good-flavored
    ripe, fresh tomatoes,
    chopped, or 2 lb 12 oz/
    1.2 kg good-quality
    canned chopped tomatoes

2 thin strips freshly pared
    orange rind

pinch hot red pepper flakes
    (optional), to taste

salt and pepper

method

1 Heat the olive oil in a large, flameproof casserole over medium heat. Add the garlic, shallots, and bell peppers and cook for 10 minutes, stirring occasionally, until the bell peppers are soft, but not brown.

2 Add the tomatoes, including the juices if using canned ones, orange rind, hot pepper flakes, if using, and salt and pepper to taste and bring to a boil. Reduce the heat to as low as possible and let simmer, uncovered, for 45 minutes, or until the liquid evaporates and the sauce thickens.

3 Purée the sauce through a mouli. Alternatively, purée in a food processor, then use a wooden spoon to press through a fine strainer. Taste and adjust the seasoning if necessary. Use at once, or cover and let chill for up to 3 days.

romesco sauce

ingredients

MAKES ABOUT ½ PINT/
300 ML/1¼ CUPS

4 large, ripe tomatoes

16 blanched almonds

3 large garlic cloves,
    unpeeled and left whole

1 dried sweet chile, such as
    ñora, soaked for 20 minutes
    and patted dry

4 dried red chiles, soaked for
    20 minutes and patted dry

pinch of sugar

¼ pint/150 ml/⅔ cup extra-
    virgin olive oil

about 2 tbsp red wine vinegar

salt and pepper

method

1 Place the tomatoes, almonds, and garlic on a baking sheet and roast in a preheated oven, 350°F/180°C, for 20 minutes, but check the almonds after about 7 minutes, because they can burn quickly; remove as soon as they are golden and giving off an aroma.

2 Peel the roasted garlic and tomatoes. Put the almonds, garlic, sweet chile, and dried red chiles in a food processor and process until finely chopped. Add the tomatoes and sugar and process again.

3 With the motor running, slowly add the olive oil through the feed tube. Add 1½ tablespoons of the vinegar and quickly process. Taste and add extra vinegar, if desired, and salt and pepper to taste.

4 Let stand for at least 2 hours, then serve at room temperature. Alternatively, cover and let chill for up to 3 days, then bring to room temperature before serving. Stir in any oil that separates before serving.

garlic mayonnaise

ingredients

**MAKES ABOUT ½ PINT/
300 ML/1 ¼ CUPS**

3–4 large garlic cloves,
    or to taste

sea salt

2 large egg yolks

1 tsp lemon juice

½ pint/300 ml/1¼ cups
    extra-virgin olive oil

salt and pepper

method

1 Mash the garlic cloves to a paste with a pinch of sea salt. Put the paste in a food processor, add the egg yolks, and lemon juice, and process.

2 With the motor still running, slowly dribble in the olive oil through the feed tube until an emulsion forms and the sauce thickens. Taste and adjust the seasoning. Cover and let chill for up to 3 days.

to finish

Spanish desserts—where do you start, they are all so good! It's always interesting to try a version of a dish that is made in several countries, so perhaps a good place to begin is with the Spanish Caramel Custard, which is similar to the French crème caramel and is the most popular dessert in Spain. You might think you've spotted another version of a French classic, crème brûlée, in the Catalan Burned Cream, but although the two desserts share a "burned" sugar topping, the custard underneath is not cooked in the Spanish recipe.

If you would love to try the Frozen Almond Cream, Lemon Sherbet with Cava, or Blood Orange Ice Cream, don't be put off if you don't have an ice-cream maker—it is perfectly possible to make a frozen dessert without one. Simply transfer the prepared mixture into a shallow freezerproof container (strain it in for the lemon sherbet) and freeze for 2 hours, or until it is beginning to freeze around the edges. At this point, beat it well with a fork, then return it to the freezer until frozen.

For a less indulgent dessert, there are some lovely fruit-based dishes—Poached Fruit, Seville Style has some intriguing flavorings—but if you decide you must go with the Spanish love of chocolate, try the Rich Chocolate Cake. It's out of this world!

frozen almond cream with hot chocolate sauce

ingredients

SERVES 4–6

6 oz/175 g/generous 1 cup
blanched almonds

1/2 pint/300 ml/1 1/4 cups
heavy cream

1/4 tsp almond extract

1/4 pint/150 ml/2/3 cup
light cream

2 oz/55 g/1/2 cup
confectioners' sugar

hot chocolate sauce

3 1/2 oz/100 g semisweet
chocolate, broken into
pieces

3 tbsp golden syrup

4 tbsp water

1 oz/25 g/2 tbsp unsalted
butter, diced

1/4 tsp vanilla extract

method

1 Toast the almonds on a baking sheet in a preheated oven, 400°F/200°C, for 7–10 minutes, stirring occasionally, until golden brown. Immediately tip onto a cutting board and let cool. Coarsely chop half the nuts and finely grind the remainder.

2 Whip the heavy cream with the almond extract until soft peaks form. Stir in the light cream and continue whipping, sifting in the sugar in 3 batches. Transfer to an ice-cream maker and freeze. When the cream is almost frozen, transfer it to a bowl, and stir in the chopped almonds. Put the mixture in a 1-lb/450-g loaf pan and smooth the top. Wrap in foil and put in the freezer for at least 3 hours.

3 To make the hot chocolate sauce, place a heatproof bowl over a pan of simmering water. Add the chocolate, syrup, and water and stir until the chocolate melts. Stir in the butter and vanilla extract until smooth.

4 To serve, dip the bottom of the loaf tin in boiling water for a couple of seconds. Invert onto a cutting board, giving a sharp shake to release the frozen cream. Coat the top and sides with the finely chopped almonds. Use a warm knife to slice into 8–12 slices. Arrange two slices on each plate and spoon over the hot chocolate sauce.

catalan burned cream

ingredients

SERVES 6

24 fl oz/750 ml/3 cups
    whole milk
1 vanilla bean, split
thinly pared rind of $1/2$ lemon
7 large egg yolks
7 oz/200 g/1 cup
    superfine sugar
3 tbsp cornstarch

method

1 A day in advance of serving, pour the milk into a pan with the vanilla bean and lemon rind. Bring to a boil, then remove from the heat and let stand for 30 minutes to infuse.

2 Put the eggs and $3^{1}/2$ oz/100 g/$^{1}/2$ cup sugar in a heatproof bowl that will fit over a pan without touching the bottom, and beat until the sugar dissolves and the mixture is creamy.

3 Return the infused milk to the heat and bring to a simmer, then stir 4 tablespoons into the cornstarch in a bowl until a smooth paste forms. Stir into the milk over medium-low heat for 1 minute. Strain the milk into the egg mixture and whisk until well blended.

4 Put the bowl over a pan of simmering water and stir the custard for 25–30 minutes until thick enough to coat the back of the spoon; the bowl must not touch the water or the eggs might scramble. Spoon the mixture into 6 x 4-inch/10-cm round cazuelas or flat white crème brûlée dishes. Let cool completely, then cover and let chill for at least 12 hours.

5 To serve, sprinkle the top of each with a thin layer of superfine sugar. Use a kitchen blowtorch to caramelize the sugar. Let stand while the caramel hardens, then serve. The caramel will remain firm for about 1 hour at room temperature; do not return to the fridge or the caramel will "melt."

spanish caramel custard

ingredients

SERVES 6

18 fl oz/500 ml/scant
    2$^1/_2$ cups whole milk
$^1/_2$ orange with 2 long, thin
    pieces of rind removed
1 vanilla bean, split, or
    $^1/_2$ tsp vanilla extract
6 oz/175 g/scant 1 cup
    superfine sugar
butter, for greasing the dish
3 large eggs, plus 2 large
    egg yolks

method

1 Pour the milk into a pan with the orange rind and vanilla bean or extract. Bring to a boil, then remove from the heat and stir in 3 oz/85 g/$^1/_2$ cup of the sugar; set aside for at least 30 minutes to infuse.

2 Meanwhile, put the remaining sugar and 4 tablespoons of water in another pan over medium-high heat. Stir until the sugar dissolves, then boil without stirring until the caramel turns deep golden brown. Immediately remove the pan from the heat and squeeze in a few drops of orange juice to stop the cooking. Pour into a lightly buttered 1$^1/_2$-pint/1-liter/5-cup soufflé dish and swirl to cover the base; set aside.

3 Return the pan of infused milk to the heat, and bring to a simmer. Beat the whole eggs and egg yolks together in a heatproof bowl. Pour the warm milk into the eggs, whisking constantly. Strain into the soufflé dish.

4 Place the soufflé dish in a roasting pan and pour in enough boiling water to come halfway up the sides of the dish. Bake in a preheated oven, 325°F/160°C, for 75–90 minutes until set and a knife inserted in the center comes out clean. Remove the soufflé dish from the roasting pan and set aside to cool completely. Cover and let chill overnight. To serve, run a metal spatula round the soufflé, then invert onto a serving plate, shaking firmly to release.

creamy chocolate puddings

ingredients

SERVES 4–6

6 oz/175 g semisweet
    chocolate, at least
    70% cocoa solids,
    broken up
1 1/2 tbsp orange juice
3 tbsp water
2 tbsp unsalted butter, diced
2 eggs, separated
1/8 tsp cream of tartar
3 tbsp superfine sugar
6 tbsp heavy cream

pistachio-orange praline

corn oil, for greasing
2 oz/55 g/generous 1/4 cup
    superfine sugar
2 oz/55 g/scant 1/2 cup
    shelled pistachios
finely grated rind of
    1 large orange

method

1 Melt the chocolate with the orange juice and water in a small pan over very low heat, stirring constantly. Remove from the heat and melt in the butter until incorporated. Using a rubber spatula, scrape the chocolate into a bowl. Beat the egg yolks until blended, then beat them into the chocolate mixture; set aside to cool.

2 In a clean bowl, whisk the egg whites with the cream of tartar until soft peaks form. Gradually beat in the sugar, 1 tablespoon at a time, beating well after each addition, until the meringue is glossy. Beat 1 tablespoon of the meringue mixture into the chocolate mixture, then fold in the rest.

3 In a separate bowl, whip the cream until soft peaks form. Fold into the chocolate mixture. Spoon into individual glass bowls or wine glasses, or 1 large serving bowl. Cover with plastic wrap and let chill for at least 4 hours.

4 To make the praline, lightly grease a baking sheet with corn oil; set aside. Put the sugar and pistachios in a small pan over medium heat. When the sugar starts to melt, stir gently until a liquid caramel forms and the nuts start popping. Pour the praline onto the baking sheet and immediately finely grate the orange rind over. Let cool until firm then coarsely chop. Just before serving, sprinkle the praline over the chocolate pudding.

rice pudding

ingredients

SERVES 4–6

1 large orange

1 lemon

1³/₄ pints/1 liter/4 cups milk

9 oz/250 g/generous 1 cup
    Spanish short-grain rice

3¹/₂ oz/100 g/¹/₂ cup
    superfine sugar

1 vanilla bean, split

pinch of salt

4 fl oz/125 ml/¹/₂ cup
    heavy cream

brown sugar, to serve (optional)

method

1 Finely grate the rinds from the orange and lemon; set aside. Rinse a heavy-bottom pan with cold water and do not dry it.

2 Put the milk and rice in the pan over medium-high heat and bring to a boil. Reduce the heat and stir in the superfine sugar, vanilla bean, orange and lemon rinds, and salt, and let simmer, stirring frequently, until the pudding is thick and creamy and the rice grains are tender: this can take up to 30 minutes, depending on how wide the pan is.

3 Remove the vanilla bean and stir in the cream. Serve at once, sprinkled with brown sugar, if desired, or let cool completely, cover, and let chill until required. (The pudding will thicken as it cools, so stir in a little extra milk, if necessary.)

"jeweled" honey mousses

ingredients

SERVES 6

1 large egg, plus 3 large
   egg yolks
6 oz/175 g/$^1/_2$ cup honey
10 fl oz/300 ml/1$^1/_4$ cups
   heavy cream
3 pomegranates, to serve

method

1 Line 6 ramekins with pieces of plastic wrap large enough to extend over the tops; set aside.

2 Put the whole egg, egg yolks, and honey in a large bowl and beat until blended and fluffy. Put the heavy cream in another bowl and beat until stiff peaks form. Fold the cream into the egg-and-honey mixture.

3 Equally divide the mixture between the ramekins, then fold the excess plastic wrap over the top of each. Place in the freezer for at least 8 hours until firm. These mousses can be served directly from the freezer, because the texture isn't solid.

4 To serve, unfold the plastic wrap, then invert each ramekin onto a serving plate and remove the ramekin and plastic wrap. Cut the pomegranates in half and hold one half over a mousse in turn. Use your other hand to tap firmly on the base of the pomegranate, so the seeds fall over the mousse. Serve at once.

lemon sherbet with cava

ingredients

SERVES 4–6

3–4 lemons

9 fl oz/250 ml/scant 1¼ cups water

7 oz/200 g/1 cup superfine sugar

1 bottle Spanish cava, chilled, to serve

method

1 Roll the lemons on the counter, pressing firmly, which helps to extract as much juice as possible. Pare off a few strips of rind and set aside for decoration, then finely grate the rind from 3 lemons. Squeeze the juice from as many of the lemons as necessary to give 6 fl oz/175 ml/ ¾ cup.

2 Put the water and sugar in a heavy-bottom pan over medium-high heat and stir to dissolve the sugar. Bring to a boil, without stirring, and boil for 2 minutes. Remove from the heat, stir in the lemon rind, cover, and let stand for 30 minutes, or until cool.

3 When the mixture is cool, stir in the lemon juice. Strain into an ice-cream maker and freeze according to the manufacturer's instructions. (Alternatively, strain the mixture into a freezerproof container and freeze for 2 hours, or until mushy and freezing round the edges. Tip into a bowl and beat. Return to the freezer and repeat the process twice more.) Remove the sherbet from the freezer to soften 10 minutes before serving.

4 To serve, scoop into 4–6 tall glasses, decorate with the reserved rind, if using, and top up with cava.

blood orange ice cream

ingredients

SERVES 4–6

3 large blood oranges, washed

3 fl oz/85 ml/^{1}/$_3$ cup lowfat milk

3 fl oz/85 ml/^{1}/$_3$ cup light cream

4^1/$_2$ oz/125 g/generous ^{5}/$_8$ cup superfine sugar

4 large egg yolks

16 fl oz/450 ml/2 cups heavy cream

^{1}/$_8$ tsp vanilla extract

method

1 Thinly pare the rind from 2 of the oranges, reserving a few strips for decoration, and finely grate the rind from the third. Squeeze the oranges to give 4 fl oz/125 ml/ ^{1}/$_2$ cup juice and set aside.

2 Pour the milk and cream into a pan with the pared orange rind. Bring to a boil, then remove from the heat; set aside to infuse for at least 30 minutes.

3 Put the sugar and egg yolks in a heatproof bowl that fits over the pan without touching the bottom and beat until thick and creamy.

4 Return the milk mixture to the heat and bring to a simmer. Pour the milk onto the eggs and whisk until well blended. Rinse the pan and add a small amount of water. Place over medium heat and bring the water to a simmer. Reduce the heat. Put the bowl on top and stir for about 20 minutes until a thick custard forms that coats the back of the spoon; the water must not touch the bottom of the bowl or the eggs might scramble.

5 Strain the mixture into a clean bowl. Stir in the finely grated orange rind and set aside for 10 minutes. Stir in the reserved juice, heavy cream, and vanilla extract. Transfer to an ice-cream maker and freeze following the manufacturer's instructions. Decorate with strips of the reserved rind.

pan-fried milk

ingredients

MAKES 25

peanut or other flavorless oil

1 pint/600 ml/2^1/$_2$ cups
    whole milk

1 cinnamon stick

1 strip of lemon rind,
    without any white pith

2 large eggs plus 1 large
    egg yolk

3^1/$_2$ oz/100 g/^{1}/$_2$ cup
    superfine sugar

2 oz/55 g/scant ^{1}/$_2$ cup
    all-purpose flour,
    plus extra for dusting

1^1/$_4$ oz/35 g/scant ^{1}/$_4$ cup
    cornstarch

1 tsp vanilla extract

olive oil

extra superfine sugar and
    cinnamon, to decorate

method

1 Pour the milk into a pan with the cinnamon stick and lemon rind. Bring to a boil, remove from the heat, and let infuse for 30 minutes.

2 Put the eggs, egg yolk, sugar, flour, cornstarch, and vanilla extract in a bowl and beat until smooth. Return the milk mixture to the heat and bring to a simmer. Pour the milk onto the egg mixture and whisk until well blended. Return to the pan and bring to a boil, stirring, then reduce the heat and let simmer for 2–3 minutes until the custard thickens.

3 Pour the custard into a 12 x 9-inch/30 x 23-cm shallow cake pan, lined with foil and lightly greased with oil, and use a wet spatula to smooth the surface. Let cool completely, then cover. Let chill for 2–3 hours, then invert onto a cutting board and peel off the foil. Cut on the diagonal to make 25 triangles. Dust the triangles in flour and shake off any excess.

4 Heat 2 inches/5 cm of oil in a heavy-bottom skillet over high heat to 350°F/180°C. Add 5–6 custard triangles at a time, without overcrowding the skillet, and cook for 45 seconds. Turn them over with a spatula or slotted spoon; continue cooking until golden brown. Transfer to crumpled paper towels and drain well. Repeat in batches with the remaining triangles. Serve sprinkled with the extra sugar and cinnamon.

deep-fried pastries

ingredients

MAKES 16–20

3$\frac{1}{2}$ oz/100 g/scant $\frac{3}{4}$ cup
 all-purpose flour

3 tbsp unsalted butter, melted

1 tbsp Spanish cream sherry

$\frac{1}{2}$ tsp vanilla extract

pinch of salt

1 small egg, beaten very lightly

olive oil, for deep-frying

to decorate

2 tbsp confectioners' sugar

$\frac{1}{2}$ tsp ground cinnamon

pinch of ground ginger

method

1 Put the flour in a bowl and make a well in the center. Add the butter, cream sherry, vanilla extract, salt, and 1 tablespoon of the egg, and mix together until a dough forms. Knead the dough in the bowl until it is smooth. Shape into a ball and wrap in plastic wrap; set aside at room temperature for 15 minutes.

2 On a lightly floured counter roll out half the dough very thinly. Use a 2$\frac{1}{4}$-inch/5.5-cm fluted cookie cutter to cut out 8–10 circles, re-rolling the trimmings. Repeat with the remaining dough.

3 Heat 2 inches/5 cm oil in a heavy-bottom skillet over high heat to 350°F/180°C or until a cube of day-old bread turns brown in 35 seconds. Add 5–6 dough circles, without overcrowding the skillet and deep-fry for 45 seconds, turn them over with a large slotted spoon, and continue cooking until the circles are puffed on both sides and golden brown. Transfer to crumpled paper towels and drain very well. Take care: they are delicate and can break easily. Repeat with the remaining dough circles.

4 While the pastries are hot, mix the confectioners' sugar, cinnamon, and ginger together. Use a fine strainer and sift the mixture over the warm pastries.

almond tart

ingredients

MAKES 1 X 10-INCH/
25-CM TART

pie dough

10 oz/280 g/2 cups
    all-purpose flour
$5^{1}/_{2}$ oz/150 g/generous
    $^{3}/_{4}$ cup superfine sugar
1 tsp finely grated lemon rind
pinch of salt
$5^{1}/_{2}$ oz/150 g unsalted butter,
    chilled and cut into
    small dice
1 medium egg, beaten lightly
1 tbsp chilled water

6 oz/175 g unsalted butter,
    at room temperature
6 oz/175 g/generous $^{3}/_{4}$ cup
    superfine sugar
3 large eggs
6 oz/175 g/generous
    $1^{1}/_{2}$ cups finely
    ground almonds
2 tsp all-purpose flour
1 tbsp finely grated orange rind
$^{1}/_{2}$ tsp almond extract
confectioners' sugar,
    to decorate
sour cream (optional), to serve

method

1 To make the pie dough, put the flour, sugar, lemon rind, and salt in a bowl. Rub or cut in the butter until the mixture resembles fine bread crumbs. Combine the egg and water, then slowly pour into the flour, stirring with a fork until a coarse mass forms. Shape into a ball and let chill for at least 1 hour.

2 Roll out the pie dough on a lightly floured counter until $^{1}/_{8}$ inch/3 mm thick. Use to line a greased 10-inch/25-cm tart pan. Return to the refrigerator for at least 15 minutes, then cover the pastry shell with foil and fill with pie weights or dried beans. Place in a preheated oven, 425°F/ 220°C, and bake for 12 minutes. Remove the pie weights and foil and return the pastry shell to the oven for 4 minutes to dry the base. Remove from the oven and reduce the oven temperature to 400°F/200°C.

3 Meanwhile, make the filling. Beat the butter and sugar until creamy. Beat in the eggs, 1 at a time. Add the almonds, flour, orange rind, and almond extract, and beat until blended.

4 Spoon the filling into the pastry shell and smooth the surface. Bake for 30–35 minutes until the top is golden and the tip of a knife inserted in the center comes out clean. Let cool completely on a wire rack, then dust with sifted confectioners' sugar. Serve with a spoonful of sour cream, if desired.

rich chocolate cake

ingredients

MAKES 10–12 SLICES

3¹/₂ oz/100 g/generous
    ¹/₂ cup raisins
finely grated rind and juice
    of 1 orange
6 oz/175 g butter, diced, plus
    extra for greasing the pan
3¹/₂ oz/100 g semisweet
    chocolate, at least
    70% cocoa solids,
    broken up
4 large eggs, beaten
3¹/₂ oz/100 g/¹/₂ cup
    superfine sugar
1 tsp vanilla extract
2 oz/55 g/scant ¹/₂ cup
    all-purpose flour
2 oz/55 g/generous ¹/₂ cup
    ground almonds
¹/₂ tsp baking powder
pinch salt
2 oz/55 g/scant ¹/₂ cup
    blanched almonds,
    toasted and chopped
confectioners' sugar, sifted,
    to decorate

method

1 Put the raisins in a small bowl, add the orange juice, and let soak for 20 minutes. Line a deep 10-inch/25-cm round cake pan with a removable bottom with waxed paper and grease the paper; set aside.

2 Melt the butter and chocolate together in a small pan over medium heat, stirring. Remove from the heat and set aside to cool.

3 Using an electric mixer beat the eggs, sugar, and vanilla together for about 3 minutes until light and fluffy. Stir in the cooled chocolate mixture.

4 Drain the raisins if they haven't absorbed all the orange juice. Sift over the flour, ground almonds, baking powder, and salt. Add the raisins, orange rind, and almonds, and fold everything together.

5 Spoon into the cake pan and smooth the surface. Bake in a preheated oven, 350°F/ 180°C, for about 40 minutes, or until a toothpick inserted into the center comes out clean and the cake starts to come away from the side of the pan. Let cool in the pan for 10 minutes, then remove from the pan and let cool completely on a wire rack. Dust with confectioners' sugar before serving.

almond cookies

ingredients

MAKES ABOUT 60

5¹/₂ oz/150 g butter, at room
temperature
5¹/₂ oz/150 g/generous
³/₄ cup superfine sugar
4 oz/115 g/generous ³/₄ cup
all-purpose flour
1 oz/25 g/generous ¹/₄ cup
ground almonds
pinch of salt
2³/₄ oz/75 g/generous ¹/₂ cup
blanched almonds,
toasted lightly and
chopped finely
finely grated rind of
1 large lemon
4 medium egg whites

method

1 Put the butter and sugar into a bowl and beat until light and fluffy. Sift over the flour, ground almonds, and salt, tipping in any ground almonds left in the strainer. Use a large metal spoon to fold in the chopped almonds and lemon rind.

2 In a separate, spotlessly clean bowl, whisk the egg whites until soft peaks form. Fold the egg whites into the almond mixture.

3 Drop small teaspoonfuls of the cookie mixture onto 1 or more well-greased baking sheets, spacing them well apart. (You might need to cook in batches.) Bake in a preheated oven, 350°F/180°C, for 15–20 minutes until the cookies are golden brown on the edges. Transfer to a wire rack to cool completely. Continue baking until all the mixture is used. Store in an airtight container for up to 1 week.

musicians' bars

ingredients

**MAKES 3 BARS; EACH
BAR SERVES 4–6**

peanut or other flavorless oil,
    for greasing
10^1/$_2$ oz/300 g/generous
    2 cups mixed nuts, such
    as blanched or
    unblanched almonds,
    slivered almonds, skinned
    hazelnuts, salted or
    unsalted skinned peanuts,
    and salted or unsalted
    pecans
3^1/$_2$ oz/100 g/generous
    ^{1}/$_2$ cup raisins
2 oz/55 g/generous ^{1}/$_2$ cup
    ready-to-eat dried
    apricots, figs, or dates,
    chopped very finely
2 oz/55 g/^{1}/$_2$ cup pine nuts

caramel

1 lb 2 oz/500 g/generous
    2^1/$_2$ cups superfine sugar
5 fl oz/150 ml/^{2}/$_3$ cup water
^{1}/$_8$ tsp white wine vinegar

method

1 Generously grease a 12 x 9-inch/30 x 23-cm baking pan and a large chef's knife with the oil; set both aside. Combine the nuts and fruit in a bowl.

2 Put the sugar, water, and vinegar in a heavy-bottom pan over medium-high heat, stirring to dissolve the sugar. Bring to a boil, then boil, without stirring, for 20–25 minutes until the caramel reaches 350°F/175°C on a sugar thermometer, or turns a rich amber color. Remove from the heat, stir in the fruit and nuts, and immediately pour into the prepared baking pan. Work very quickly, using a wet spatula to spread the mixture evenly.

3 Let the caramel stand for a few minutes to set until firm but not too brittle to cut. Invert the caramel bar onto a sheet of greased waxed paper and use the oiled knife to cut into 3 slabs each measuring 4 x 9 inches/ 10 x 23 cm. Let cool until brittle, then wrap each in foil and store for up to 1 week.

valencia caramel oranges

ingredients

SERVES 4–6

4 large, juicy oranges

9 oz/250 g/generous
   1¼ cups superfine sugar

10 fl oz/300 ml/1¼ cups
   water

4–6 tbsp slivered almonds,
   toasted, to serve

method

1 Working over a heatproof bowl to catch any juices, and using a small serrated knife, pare the oranges, taking care not to leave any of the bitter-tasting pith. Use the knife to remove the orange segments, cutting between the membranes. Squeeze the empty membranes over the bowl to extract as much juice as possible; discard the membranes and set the segments and juice aside.

2 Put the sugar and 5 fl oz/150 ml/^{2}/$_3$ cup of the water into a small, heavy-bottom pan over medium-high heat. Stir until the sugar dissolves, then bring to a boil and continue boiling, without stirring, until the syrup turns a rich golden brown.

3 Pour the remaining water into the pan (stand back because the caramel will splatter). Stir again until the caramel dissolves. Remove from the heat and let the caramel cool slightly, then pour over the oranges. Stir to blend the orange juice into the caramel. Let the oranges cool completely, then cover with plastic wrap and let chill for at least 2 hours before serving.

4 Just before serving, sprinkle the caramel oranges with the toasted slivered almonds.

poached fruit, seville style

ingredients

SERVES 4–6

syrup

1/2 tsp fennel seeds

1/2 tsp coriander seeds

1/4 tsp black peppercorns

7 oz/200 g/1 cup
   superfine sugar

8 fl oz/225 ml/1 cup
   red wine, such as Rioja

8 fl oz/225 ml/1 cup water

3 tbsp freshly squeezed
   orange juice

2 tbsp freshly squeezed
   lemon juice

2 tbsp Spanish cream sherry

3 cloves

1 cinnamon stick

12 tender apricots, halved
   and pitted

2 tbsp slivered almonds,
   toasted, to decorate

method

1 First, make the red wine syrup. Put the fennel and coriander seeds and peppercorns in a heavy-bottom pan over high heat and dry-fry for up to about 1 minute until they start to give off an aroma. Immediately tip them out of the pan to stop the cooking. Put in a mortar and lightly crush.

2 Put the sugar, wine, water, orange and lemon juices, sherry, and all the spices into a heavy-bottom pan over medium-high heat, stirring to dissolve the sugar. Bring to a boil, without stirring, and let bubble for 5 minutes.

3 Add the fruit and let simmer for 6–8 minutes until tender. Remove the pan from the heat and transfer to a bowl of iced water and let cool. When cool enough to handle, remove the apricots, and peel. Cover and let chill until required.

4 Meanwhile, return the juices to the heat and boil until the syrup thickens and the flavors become more concentrated. Remove from the heat and let cool.

5 When ready to serve, place the fruit in serving bowls, spoon the syrup over, then sprinkle with slivered almonds.

baked apricots with honey

ingredients

SERVES 4

butter, for greasing

4 apricots, each cut in half
    and pitted

4 tbsp slivered almonds

4 tbsp honey

pinch ground ginger or
    grated nutmeg

vanilla ice cream,
    to serve (optional)

method

1 Lightly butter an ovenproof dish large enough to hold the apricot halves in a single layer.

2 Arrange the apricot halves in the dish, cut sides up. Sprinkle with the almonds and drizzle the honey over. Dust with the spice.

3 Bake in a preheated oven, 400°F/200°C, for 12–15 minutes until the apricots are tender and the almonds golden. Remove from the oven and serve at once, with ice cream on the side, if desired.

dates stuffed with spanish marzipan

ingredients

MAKES 12–14

spanish marzipan

2¹/₂ oz/70 g/generous ¹/₄ cup confectioners' sugar, plus extra for dusting

2¹/₂ oz/70 g/scant ³/₄ cup ground almonds

¹/₄ tsp almond extract

12–14 ready-to-eat dates

method

1 To make the Spanish marzipan, sift the confectioners' sugar then mix with the ground almonds in a bowl. Sprinkle over the almond extract. Gradually add a little water, ¹/₄ teaspoon at a time, until the mixture comes together and can be pressed into a ball.

2 Knead the marzipan in your hands and then on a counter dusted with confectioners' sugar until it is smooth. It is now ready to be used, or can be wrapped in plastic wrap and stored in the fridge for up to 3 days.

3 To stuff the dates, use a small knife to slice along the length of each, then open out and pull out the pit. Break off a small piece of the marzipan and mold it into a "log," pressing it into the date. Arrange the dates on a plate and serve with coffee after dinner.